The Dominant Culture:

Living in the Promised Land

Martin Murphy

The Dominant Culture: Living in the Promised Land

Dedicated to Christians, past, present, and future
for taking godly worldviews
into the culture

Acknowledgments

This exposition of Judges would not have been possible without the perspective of a wide range of life principles. The format of this book does not follow the style of an academic monograph; however, considerable research went into the preparation and writing. The lectures and instruction of my Old Testament professors in Bible College and Seminary laid the foundation for all my understanding of the Old Testament. Dr. Bryan Beyer (Columbia International University) and Dr. Richard Pratt (President of Third Millennium Ministries, formally Old Testament Professor, Reformed Theological Seminary) had a tremendous influence on my understanding of the Old Testament. However, any errors in my exegesis and exposition of the doctrine of the text are my own.

Preface

This book resonates with my life experience. It is a book to muse, because it is about real life. Reflecting on the work involved, my first thought was how gracious God has been to allow me to write and publish ten books. My second thought was "what would my mother have thought about this landmark?" She died when I was about six weeks old. I was told that she met with ladies in the church and enjoyed many good prayer services together. In a church paper the following is an excerpt from her eulogy. "She so sweetly gave her baby to God, and prayed so earnestly that he would prove to be a blessing in this world." I hope that, if not in my lifetime, my books will be a blessing to someone.

The Dominant Culture: Living in the Promised Land, describes two distinctive, but related cultures; one godly and the other ungodly. The Israelites lived in the Promised Land, but they were not the dominant culture. The church should learn the principles that the Israelites failed to learn about how to engage in the dominant culture. This book was written to a church in a cultural crisis.

Table of Contents

Introduction

The abandonment of the debate table is the mark of a senseless society suffering from cultural chaos. The dignity, honor, and order of our civil and political lives depend on intelligent human discourse. The evangelical church, in the early days of the United States, generated a host of intellectual giants like Jonathan Edwards and Robert L. Dabney. They courageously and honorably defended the principles found in the infallible Word of God, using the rules of intelligent human discourse to present the truth. They were logicians, philosophers, theologians, political and economic theorists. They used tongues of persuasion and the power of the pen to champion the Christian culture. Did their logic, philosophy, theology and political theory disappear when these men went to their eternal Sabbath? No, their concepts and ideas are very much alive, but the creeping conspiracies of modernity and the abrupt emergence of post modernity overshadow the principles of truth and the laws of intelligent discourse.

Modernity has been described by one Christian sociologist as, "the character and system of the world produced by the forces of modernization and development." Even though modernity is associated with the secular (the here and now), modernity is more a concept than a period of time. The fourteenth century scholastics spoke of the *via moderna*, the modern way, long before the eighteenth century enlightenment. Yet there is a sense in which I agree with other scholars who believe that modernity raged from the storming of the Bastille to the fall of the Berlin wall. Modernity is the monster produced by the forces of its age such as hedonism, narcissism, pragmatism, individualism, and especially relativism. The love of self naturally leads to the love of practicality and a hatred for truth.

The postmodern has replaced the modern. Like modernity, postmodernity is more a concept than a time period, but postmodernity seems to have come to prominence in the middle of the twentieth century. Postmodern architecture such as elegant shopping malls replaced modern architecture on the old down town square. The popular has replaced the ideal. The postmodern world is more interested in a purely subjective interpretation of the world, than employing inductive and deductive argumentation to prove a proposition. In the postmodern world words are meaningless. Assertion has replaced proof. Image is everything. So you can easily see that the postmodern theory of interpretation was very comfortable with Immanuel Kant in the eighteenth century, since his fundamental philosophy was human autonomy. But more to the point, the postmodern concept has rejected tradition in favor of the alleged creative forces of subjectivity. The postmodern concept has made its mark on everything from theology to quantum physics.

So, where does a civil Christian culture fit into this philosophical smorgasbord? It fits in the same place as the conventional traditional American culture fits into it. Both have drank deeply from the streams of modernity and plowed headlong into the pits of postmodernity. Christians may seek refreshment from the modern/postmodern scene. However, Christians must show their opposition and displeasure toward the cultural and political carpetbaggers who would steal the divine principles from them, if it were possible. The cultural wars and statism must be seen as the enemy if Christians expect to save the Christian culture for the coming generations.

Those who call themselves politically correct have extorted ungodly worldviews into public spectacles for the purpose of diverting attention from the real issues of life. Now the puzzle begins to take shape as we see that utilitarian and political strategies replace ethics and morals. The result is that the state supposedly provides all the answers of life.

Statism is not a theory. It is a way of life. *Webster's Dictionary* describes statism as, "The principle or policy of concentrating extensive economic, political, and related controls in the state at the cost of individual liberty." The philosopher/apologist, Francis Shaffer, lectured against statism back in the 1970's. Statism is an artificial form of *docetism* (*docetism* refers to that which appears to be real, but does not exist in reality). The promises of statism are empty and are in stark contrast to the natural order of any society. What began as the natural order in our civil society has now descended to an unnatural order. The fundamental society of the human race is found in a conjugal society. A man and a woman produce offspring within a covenant community. The formation of that society is not based on utilitarianism, pragmatism, or egalitarianism. It is the society that respects and honors the authority of a triune God and bases the form of government on an understanding of the ordinances of creation. Marriage, work, and worship are the fundamental ordinances of a natural conjugal society. They are the principles embraced by a Christian way of life. Statism is repulsive to a Christian culture. Are there elements of statism that may aid us in our society? Absolutely not! John Calvin left this wise piece of advice concerning worship which principle applies to the stabilization of any culture. Calvin said, "There is no end, when men once depart ever so little from the pure worship of the only true God; for when anything is blended with it one error immediately produces another" (*John Calvin Commentaries*, Jeremiah 11:13). The analogy, which is apropos to my discussion, is that, "one error immediately produces another." Statism is an evil to be resisted, because the slightest inclination toward it will likely provoke a greater inclination. Within a few generations the product is full blown. In 1934, Dr. J. Gresham Machen commented on statism relative to education:

> It is very sad that all the struggle of humanity toward enlightenment and freedom should succeed only in producing reaction and slavery like that which is involved in the modern paternalistic State. (*Education, Christianity, and the State*, by J. Gresham Machen, p. 134-135).

Statism and the paternalistic State are synonyms. The paternalistic State wants to govern every detail of the subjects under it, thus turning the state into a god.

This book is about cultural recovery which means a recovery of truth. When I use the word truth, I have in mind a conceptual idea that truth is reality and that truth affirms itself aesthetically, reasonably, and sensibly. Truth reveals itself in beauty, wisdom, rationality, and in the world of sense experience. Does that mean that ethics and morals are exempt from the meaning established for truth? Absolutely not! In fact, an ethical system and the functions of morality are manifested (not established) in a reasonable world with aesthetically and sensibly derived propositions from the ultimate truth, the Word of God.

Cultural recovery will require a passion for truth. We have to remember how far we have fallen into the arms of modernity and postmodernity. We have to remember, with rare exceptions, this and previous generations have not understood or even studied the logic of language. We have to remember, they have been taught that truth is relative. This generation learned to make decisions based on emotional subjectivity, rather than rational objectivity. God created rational human beings naturally inclined to truth. Professor David Wells said, "It is not theology alone in which I am interested but theology that is driven by a passion for truth."

By analogy, I can say the same about culture, politics, or economics. We must have a passion for truth.

Cultural recovery will require a passion for absolute truth. The neo-dark age before us is prefaced with the postmodern hermeneutic called deconstructionism. It is an interpretative device that allows one to deconstruct written literary forms and reconstruct them so that they become meaningful to the interpreter. This is not the same as relativism, because the meaning is absolute for the interpreter, but it certainly seems kin to relativism to me. I have heard many people say, "truth is relative." I remember talking to a preacher (he had a Master's degree in divinity) over twenty years ago about a particular Bible doctrine. When I objected to his interpretation of Scripture I began to develop my arguments logically, biblically, and apparently compellingly because he finally said, "it really doesn't make any difference." Then I asked him this question: "Do you believe that both of us have found the truth, even though the views are opposite, and that we can hold these two opposing views in harmony at the same time and in the same relationship?" He said, "yes!" I said, "Then, our conversation (debate) is useless and truth is relative." He agreed and we have had no real or intelligent conversation since. Truth cannot be relative. Truth is absolute. Truth is absolutely, absolute.

Christians must understand the concept of truth and teach the present culture the difference between truth and error, so they may experience the difference between freedom and tyranny. Even the social compact theorist, John Locke, said, "Tyranny is the exercise of power beyond right." If we do not understand what is "right," we will ultimately be the subjects of tyranny. Our Christian forefathers were men of intellectual and theological acumen. They realized that truth was an attribute of God and a gift to the human race. The intellectual and godly men from previous generations understood that mercy was from the Lord and that His lovingkindness and His truth continually preserved His people. We look to the Lord for His divine help, as we work toward a biblical cultural recovery.

The word culture from the Latin *cultura* refers to land and life associated with it such as tilling the soil. The related Latin word *cultus* refers to the actions and worship associated with life. The English dictionary provides a wide range of nuances for the word culture. One definition is "the total of the inherited ideas, beliefs, values and knowledge, which constitute the shared basis of social action." *The Dictionary of Philosophy*, edited by Dagobert D. Runes, describes culture as "the intrinsic value of society." H. Richard Niebuhr wrote a book published under the title Christ and Culture. He described culture from a Christian perspective. "It [culture] comprises language, habits, ideas, beliefs, customs, social organization, inherited artifacts, technical processes and values." His definition was derived from an article entitled "Culture" in the *Encyclopedia of Social Sciences* written by Bronislaw Malinowski. For clarity and consistency, the word culture throughout this book refers to "a way of life."

Individuals and groups within a culture will formulate worldviews to understand and influence the culture in which they live. Every aspect of culture will be influenced by worldviews. Conflicting worldviews normally occur because of individual preferences competing in the public sector in terms of demands. They often turn into cultural wars. The cultural wars are the battles that are being fought in the public arena in this postmodern culture over the important issues of life. Cultural wars are those controversies that divide the American public with reference to politics, art, education, law, family and a host of other issues.

God created a perfect culture and "then the Lord God took the man and put him in the Garden of Eden to tend and keep it" (Genesis 2:15). Man disobeyed the Lord and tried to come up with a better culture. The fall of man introduced cultural distinctions; one was godly and the other was ungodly.

God has always been generous to give His people a distinctive culture. After God brought His people out of an ungodly culture in Egypt and from the bondage of that ungodly culture, He gave them a new culture. He gave them a new way of life and promised them land to go with it. God gave them a new leader named Joshua. God told Joshua to be strong and courageous and observe the whole law of God, which was a godly culture. The twelve tribes of Israel conquered and settled in the land that God had promised them, but they did not destroy the ungodly culture as God had instructed them. God commanded His people to occupy the land and exterminate the Canaanite culture and religion, but the people did not heed God's command. At the end of Joshua's life, the Lord God spoke to His people with a warning.

> Therefore take careful heed to yourselves, that you love the LORD your God. Or else, if indeed you do go back, and cling to the remnant of these nations— these that remain among you—and make marriages with them, and go in to them and they to you, know for certain that the LORD your God will no longer drive out these nations from before you. But they shall be snares and traps to you, and scourges on your sides and thorns in your eyes, until you perish from this good land which the LORD your God has given you. (Joshua 23:11-13)

"Now therefore," he said, "put away the foreign gods which are among you, and incline your heart to the LORD God of Israel" (Joshua 24:23). This book is an exposition of the book of Judges. It is a book about cultural chaos and the hard times associated with the ugliness of sin. It will show how unbelief, hypocrisy and human frailty invades the culture with ungodly worldviews. The book of Judges lays the framework for the future religious and political life of the nation of Israel and ultimately the church of all ages.

A common religious bond united the assembly of Israelite tribes. The focal point of this *cultus* was a central sanctuary located first at Shechem, then at Shiloh, then at Bethel, and finally back to Shiloh. The fundamental characterization of life during the period of the Judges was that of a confederation. Unfortunately, the political and military confederation was weak. Their religious life failed to recognize the principle of monarchy.

The principle of confederation joins people and groups together for common purposes by mutual agreement. They have individual personalities, but work together for a common purpose. The civil dimension of life is best ordered by the principle of confederation. Social, political, and economic expressions of any culture ought to have a common purpose by uncommon people. The book of Judges describes the recurring cycle of God's people from degeneration to spiritual revival. The book of Judges is the descriptive history of God's people again being replicated in our postmodern culture.

The nation of Israel ought to have adopted the principle of monarchy as a way of life for theological and moral purposes. "For God is the King of all the earth" (Psalm 47:7). Joshua diligently instructed God's people to maintain the monarchial principle in their spiritual lives.

> When you have transgressed the covenant of the LORD your God, which He commanded you, and have gone and served other gods, and bowed down to them, then the anger of the LORD will burn against

you, and you shall perish quickly from the good land which He has given you. (Joshua 23:16)

The good land was the Promised Land, a land filled with milk and honey. However, the dominant culture was an ungodly culture.

Joshua died and the people of God turned to their King asking, "Who shall be first to go up for us against the Canaanites to fight against them?" (Judges 1:1). Judah was chosen and Judah confederated with his brother Simeon. Although the Israelites were in the land they still did not possess it. The book of Judges reveals the chaos of a people who failed to apply the principles that God set before them. Like the people in the Old Testament, Christians today are disenfranchised from those same principles.

God gave Israel a culture. It was a way of life based on eternal principles. The people of God join together in a confederacy under the rule of an eternal perfect Monarch to fulfill the cultural mandate from God. He created rational creatures (human beings) to rule over the rest of the natural world (See Genesis 1:28; 9:1-2). Cultural chaos entered when man broke God's covenant. Like the children of Israel occupied the land, Christians occupy the culture, but they do not possess it.

The book of Judges covers about 350 years of history; 350 years vacillating from victory to defeat; 350 years of cultural chaos. They were victorious when they followed the principles given by God. They were defeated when they assumed the principle "I am and there is no one else besides me" (Isaiah 48:10). They were defeated because of their pride and arrogance from earlier victories, such as they experienced at Jericho. Living on the glory of past victories will finally end in defeat. Another reason the Israelites were defeated is that they were faithless in the face of trouble. The modern church follows the same pattern that Israel followed.

9

Every person on this planet is under the influence of a culture. Every culture has cultural elites, the people who have the greatest influence over a particular culture. It may be a tyrant like the lord of Bezek (Judges 1:5-7) or some other name in recent history. Philosophers, theologians, educators, politicians, actors, or anyone of celebrity status will influence culture. Ungodly rational creatures without Jesus Christ at the center of their culture will have an ungodly influence. Without Jesus Christ, ungodly worldviews will invade the culture. Chaos becomes a way of life. Godly rational creatures with Jesus Christ at the center of their culture will have a godly influence. It will be a culture of peace and harmony as individuals confederate for mission and ministry and submit to the rule of one King of kings.

1. Cultural Ownership

And when Joshua had dismissed the people, the children of Israel went each to his own inheritance to possess the land.

Judges 2:6

Civil, social, and religious life during the period of the Judges represents the culture for God's people during 350 years of history. It is a story of hills and valleys in the life of God's covenant community. It reflects a life of victory and defeat. There were two cultures on the same piece of property; one was a godly culture and the other was an ungodly culture.

God gave His people a way of life. They were instructed and expected to "fear the Lord, serve Him in sincerity and in truth, and put away the gods which your fathers served on the other side of the River and in Egypt. Serve the Lord!" (Joshua 24:14). However, the Israelites loved the false gods and the culture of the Canaanites. The Israelites choose the culture of unbelief, hypocrisy and rebellion.

Why did the Israelites fall in love with the Canaanite culture? The answer is simple. The presence of the Canaanites and their way of life appealed to the natural senses of the Israelites. God commanded the Israelites to destroy the Canaanite culture and religion, but like most sinners, they thought they knew what was right for the culture.

Professing Christians in the postmodern world might have some difficulty understanding life during the period of the Judges. During the period of the Judges, the church and the state were unified, in principle, by a divine mandate from God. As a state, the different tribes of Israel were bound together for the well-being of this earthly life. The preservation of life was described in terms of "you shall love your neighbor as yourself" (Leviticus 19:18). As a church, Israel was commanded to worship the one true and living God. God was the cosmic monarch with absolute power and authority over His subjects.

The contemporary church also lives in an ungodly culture. God has given His church the same principles He gave to Israel. If the violates these fundamental principles, they will suffer, and find sorrow instead of salvation. There is hope for Christians living in an ungodly culture. God's covenant promises still stand.

God sent Moses and Joshua after him to warn God's people to obey the Lord. The warning given to the congregation in the wilderness is the same warning that has consequences for every generation of God's people.

> Take heed to yourself, lest you make a covenant with the inhabitants of the land where you are going, lest it be a snare in your midst. But you shall destroy their altars, break their sacred pillars, and cut down their wooden images (for you shall worship no other god, for the LORD, whose name is Jealous, is a jealous God), lest you make a covenant with the inhabitants of the land, and they play the harlot with their gods and make sacrifice to their gods, and one of them invites you and you eat of his sacrifice, and you take of his daughters for your sons, and his daughters play the harlot with their gods and make your sons play the harlot with their gods (Exodus 34:12-16).

The people who originally heard those words were dead, but God was faithful to remind the new generation of Israelites that adopting any way of life other than His way was a bad choice. God sent an angel to warn the new generation of Israelites (Judges 2:1). Christians in the modern era are enamored with the popular notion "I got a word from the Lord or I'm waiting on a word from the Lord." The Lord has given His people many words. Depending on which translation of the Bible one uses, there is somewhere around 750,000 words from the Lord. Some of His words are simple to understand, but some require the use of God's provision, which are rationality and intelligence. Unfortunately, the use of both of those will require diligent effort and further inquiry.

One of the principles that God declares in the book of Judges that His people ignored is, "You shall make no covenant with the inhabitants of this land (Judges 2:1). The message was spoken to "all the children of Israel" (Judges 2:4).

It is incumbent upon Christians today not only to listen to God's Word, but also to obey God's Word. God's Word is set in stone and will not change. God said, "I will never break my covenant with you" (Judges 2:1). Unfortunately, that phrase taken out of context will end up being scrambled in the cultural chaos. For example, Liberation theology adopted almost exclusively by theological liberals is very predominant in feminist and black theology. It emphasizes deliverance from temporal bondage and alleged suffering, rather than redemption from sin.

Liberation theology is one among many of the errors found in the cultural chaos and imbedded in the postmodern church. All theology begins with a biblical understanding of divine covenants. God is a covenant maker, but His covenants are always accompanied with stipulations. Man will either keep the covenant or break the covenant. For instance, the Bible begins with God making a covenant with Adam.

> Then the LORD God took the man and put him in the Garden of Eden to tend and keep it. And the LORD God commanded the man, saying, "Of every tree of

the garden you may freely eat; but of the tree of the knowledge of good and evil you shall not eat, for in the day that you eat of it you shall surely die. (Genesis 2:15-17)

Then the masterful charmer tempted Eve to break the covenant. The charming sophisticated deception of Satan charmed Eve.

The modern version of Satan's charming temptation may sound something like this, "Did God really mean such and such; surely God did not mean it." Adam broke God's covenant. It began the history of victimizationalism. No one wants to accept responsibility for sin. It is always the other person's fault. When God asked Adam why he broke covenant and ate the forbidden fruit, Adam said, "The woman whom You gave to be with me, she gave me of the tree and I ate" (Genesis 3:12). Adam blamed God, because the implication is if God had not given Adam the woman, he would not have sinned. You can shuffle the words any way you want to, but victimizationalism is the worldview that blames the sin problem on other people.

The Old Testament church heard the Word of God though the mouth of the angel, "I will never break My covenant with you" (Judges 2:1). However, the stipulation was that the people of God would not intermingle and make covenants with the inhabitants of the land God had given to His people. Instructions that are more specific were given to the congregation before they crossed the Jordon.

Now the LORD spoke to Moses in the plains of Moab by the Jordan, across from Jericho, saying, "Speak to the children of Israel, and say to them: 'When you have crossed the Jordan into the land of Canaan, then you shall drive out all the inhabitants of the land from before you, destroy all their engraved stones, destroy all their molded images, and demolish all their high places; you shall dispossess the inhabitants of the land and dwell in it, for I have given you the land to possess. And you shall divide the land by lot as an inheritance among your families; to the larger you shall give a larger inheritance, and to the smaller you shall give a smaller inheritance; there everyone's inheritance shall be whatever falls to him by lot. You shall inherit according to the tribes of your fathers. However, if you do not drive out the inhabitants of the land from before you, then it shall be that those whom you let remain shall be irritants in your eyes and thorns in your sides, and they shall harass you in the land where you dwell. Moreover it shall be that I will do to you as I thought to do to them.'" (Numbers 33:50-56)

However, the people of God disobeyed God. They co-mingled with the people of land and worshiped with the Canaanites. God's professing people have a long history of mixing ungodly cultural life with godly worship. Amos has a question for those who practice syncretism: "Can two walk together, unless they are agreed?" (Amos 3:3). The New Testament teaches the same principle. "Do not be unequally yoked together with unbelievers. For what fellowship has righteousness with lawlessness? And what communion has light with darkness? In addition, what accord has Christ with Belial? Or what part has a believer with an unbeliever?" (2 Corinthians 6:14-15). The principle idea from these and other places in Scripture is to avoid mixing ungodly doctrine and worship with godly doctrine and worship.

God told His people not to make a covenant with the inhabitants of the land. They were instructed not to co-mingle false worship with true worship. Yet, God's people were tolerant of the Canaanites. Their tolerance would disenfranchise the Israelites from their God who was their source of strength. If Christians today do not resist the devil, they will lose their strength. During the period of the Judges God warned the people of God: "their god shall be a snare to you" (Judges 2:3). The principle is interminable: tolerance leads to temptation. If Christians ignore the principle of monarchy, then they do not have a standard by which to understand the covenantal structure from God.

Whether it was the angel in the Book of Judges or the Word of God in the 21st century, the people of God will have to decide which way of life (culture) they will choose. The people of old "lifted up their voices" and "sacrificed to the Lord" (Judges 2:45). Christians today may yell and scream, but in the end will the culture own them or will they own the culture?

After the death of Joshua and all the elders of his time, there was gross apostasy in Israel. The parents did not invade and clean up the culture. The professing people of God played church and the children quit church. The people "lifted up their voices" in great sorrow, because they lived in the land; however, they were not the dominant culture.

The Lord Jesus Christ came to save His people from their sins (Matthew 1:21). His people have the great privilege to engage in the purpose, mission, and ministry of the church. They have the opportunity to fill culture with worldviews that glorify and honor the Lord Jesus Christ, the ultimate prophet, priest and king.

2. The Anger of the Lord

And the anger of the Lord was hot against Israel. So He delivered them into the hand of plunderers who despoiled them; and He sold them into the hands of their enemies all around, so that they could no longer stand before their enemies.

Judges 2:14

Acceptance is very important in a divided culture. It is the "me" world. Do not challenge me! Do not question me! Do not try to make me think! What I believe is what is important to me and I do not want anyone telling me I am wrong. It's all about ME! Yet God's Word clearly challenges us to think about the serious and real questions of life.

The Word of God uniquely challenges the people of God. It makes them ask the questions they do not like to ask. It makes them think about reality. It makes them realize there are principles that do not change. The book of Judges reveals principles that are particularly applicable to the conflict between God's plan for culture and the man's plan for culture. In just a few chapters from the book of Judges, we see the summary of Israel's history for about 300 years. It is a book about the nation of Israel as they follow a cycle of vicious rebellious history.

The first and greatest act of rebellion was not destroying the wicked dominant culture that remained in the land after the death of Joshua. Man's culture will always reject God's culture because of man's total depravity.

From the time of the Judges until the establishment of the monarchy in Israel, there was a cycle of sin, disaster, repentance, and deliverance. The book of Judges is like a history book that goes through four cycles or phases. The cycles or phases follow the same sequence over and over. Those phases are:

2. The Anger of the Lord

Phase 1 - Sin and apostasy.
Phase 2 - Disaster, punishment, and slavery.
Phase 3 - Repentance and pardon.
Phase 4 - Salvation and deliverance.

The first phase is a recurring problem because the children of Israel rebelled against the Lord.

> Then the children of Israel did evil in the sight of the LORD, and served the Baals; and they forsook the LORD God of their fathers, who had brought them out of the land of Egypt; and they followed other gods from among the gods of the people who were all around them, and they bowed down to them; and they provoked the LORD to anger. They forsook the LORD and served Baal and the Ashtoreths. (Judges 2:11-13)

"Served the Baals" literally means they worshipped the Baals. The Canaanite god named Baal was the Canaanite god believed to control rain and fertility. The Israelites were commanded not to depend on a false god for anything especially for the production of crops and increased herds. Yet the Israelites worshiped this dead god. It is called idolatry.

God's own people "forsook the Lord God of their fathers, who had brought them out of the land of Egypt." The Hebrew word translated "forsook" essentially means to abandon or desert. God's people apostatized; they left the faith. Their sin caused them to give up the culture God had given them. The principle is sin leads to false worship. It may be applied to the church in the American culture.

Idolatry is a temptation and sin of every generation. Christians must not think that the Israelites were the most repugnant, rebellious religious monsters of all history.

Idolatry is the chief sin of every person. The gravity of an ungodly culture pulls Christians to the man-centered religion of Satan. The only escape is by the finished work of Jesus Christ. It is Christ alone and His redemptive work that brings Christians to face the reality of idolatry. From birth, human beings invent idols and place them at the center of their religious world until as last they are hopelessly held captive by a whole pantheon of idols unless the Lord saves them. The principle is that culture begins at birth and will continue down a destructive path unless God's saving grace intervenes. Then a new way of life begins.

In the second phase of the history of the Judges God sends calamity and punishes His people. "The Lord delivered them into the hands of plunderers who despoiled them; and He sold them into the hands of their enemies all around, so that they could no longer stand before their enemies" (Judges 2:14). The Israelites did not understand the nature and character of God. They forgot that God and God alone is able to produce good crops or destroy crops. The Canaanite gods and their alleged reproductive powers were merely illusions. God's people also forgot that the Lord has the power to punish His people.

Israel broke her promises to obey the Lord by serving and worshipping idols. As a covenant breaker, Israel lost the promised blessings of God's covenant. The result was serious and painful. God's people were sold into the hands of their enemies. They were sold into slavery.

As much as the revisionist historians and liberals hate it, slavery is an institution ordained by God. (I discuss this concept in greater detail in chapter three.) Unbiblical slavery is a sin. Biblical slavery is not only legitimate, but under God's law may be a great blessing. It is all about understanding principles, from either a God-centered culture or a man-centered culture. Truth principles are derived from the Word of God. God's people, the nation/church in the Old

Testament, were sold into slavery, which was God's punishment for their own voluntary slavery to the Canaanite idols.

The question that baffles the minds of many professing Christians is, "Why would God sell His own people into the hands of the enemy?" The answer is really very simple. God cannot and will not tolerate evil among His people. By simple deduction, we know that the principle in Scripture is "the punishment fits the crime." He is patient and longsuffering, but His people must pray for the grace of repentance.

The more evil God's people act, the more punishment they may expect. With that in mind, think a moment about the national sins in our nation and the corporate sins in the church. As a nation, we have abandoned the biblical principle of confederacy and adopted the unbiblical principle of monarchy for the state. Centralized power, multiculturalism, and despotism are the regulating and prevalent factors in our nation. Centralized power belongs to only to the sovereign triune God. Multiculturism literally means more that one culture. God divided men into different people groups because of sin and man has not perfected himself. The Israelites tried to mix a God-centered culture with a man-centered culture. God became angry and the whole mess was a disaster. Despotism results when one or just a few people hold centralized power. If God is not the centralized power, the power is sinful and anti-biblical.

As a church, Christians have abandoned the biblical principle of monarchy and adopted the unbiblical principle of confederacy for the church. There is no democracy with truth. God is the absolute monarch who demands obedience to His Word. Churches do not come together in a common agreement for the purpose of advancing religion. Churches come together to worship and serve the living God according to His prescription. The crisis Christians face in this country and the crisis they face as the church of the Lord Jesus Christ will surely bring calamity and punishment, if they do not repent.

The church is sure to incur God's judgment if she ignores the principles God has given for a way of life, a culture. God's judgment follows from His anger. It is a causal proposition that can only be avoided if God's people repent.

Although it is an unpopular principle among many evangelicals, God does become angry with His people when they ignore His Word and live according to their own desires. During the time of the Judges, God became angry when God's people bowed down to other gods. To put this into perspective it is necessary to re-visit the Word of God. The Old Testament church "forsook the LORD God of their fathers, who had brought them out of the land of Egypt; and they followed other gods from among the gods of the people who were all around them, and they bowed down to them; and they provoked the LORD to anger" (Judges 2:12). God alone is the object of worship. The less people worship Him and the more they worship something else, the angrier God will be. The angrier God becomes, the more He will demonstrate his punishment. God became hot with anger when God's people served Baal and the Ashtoreths. (See Judges 2:14).

If Christians are deceived by the lies of Satan, then they will serve and give more interest to the things of Satan than to the things of God. The more Christians accept the lies of the Old Deceiver, the more likely they are to adopt a syncretistic worldview. Two opposing cultures will never live in harmony with each other.

> Then the anger of the Lord was hot against Israel; and He said, "Because this nation has transgressed My covenant which I commanded their father and has not heeded My voice, I also will no longer drive out be-

fore them any of the nations which Joshua left when he died... ." (Judges 2:20)

Likewise, this nation has not listened to and obeyed God. I have every reason to believe that the President of the United States thinks he is above the law of God based on several years of inconsistent, incoherent decisions and the fact that he shows little interest in a Christian culture. God's anger is evident by the downward spiral of what once was considered a great nation.

Evangelical churches in this country have angered God even more than the state. The church has bowed down to the ungodly philosophies of this age and created ignominious worldviews that are contemptible in the face of God. They have ignored God's culture and adopted man's culture and for that, God's anger is hot against the church. Unfortunately, many do not see the anger of the Lord or they simply believe their culture is better than God's culture.

The anger of the Lord should stir all God's people to faith and repentance. The Bible reveals the anger and the wrath of God coming upon His people. One of the saddest verses in the entire Bible is, "Therefore the wrath of the Lord was kindled against His people, So that He abhorred His own inheritance" (Psalm 106:40).

Christ the Savior has bought His people an eternal inheritance with His own blood. That blood calls God's people to turn from their sin in faith and repentance; Then God will deliver them from their enemy and give them an eternal Sabbath rest.

3.   Flirting With the Enemy

Thus the children of Israel dwelt among the Canaanites, the Hittites, the Amorites, the Perizzites, the Hivites, and the Jebusites. And they took their daughters to be their wives, and gave their daughters to their sons; and they served their gods.

Judges 3:5-6

God gave His people a specific way of life. It was a culture that was specifically God-centered. However, "they mingled with the Gentiles and learned their works; they served their idols, which became a snare to them" (Psalm 106:35-36). During the period of the Judges, the Old Testament congregation flirted and intermingled with the enemy. The time would come when the people of God would need someone to deliver them from their enemies. In due time, God sent His people a Judge to deliver them.

The first Judge in the book of Judges was Othniel. He was the nephew of Caleb. Moses had sent spies into the land of promise for reconnaissance and to report about the dominant culture. Caleb was one of the spies. It was Joshua and Caleb who were confident of Israel's ability to take the Promised Land. Caleb was about 85 years old when he was given his portion in the Promised Land. Othniel was the next generation after Caleb. So, his offspring would have produced the first babies born in the enemy occupied territory.

This period of time in the history of Israel was the degeneration of a generation. The Bible mentions an unspecified number of young Israelites who did not have the necessary military skills to fight against the enemy (Judges 3:2).

The Israelites expected physical engagement in warfare to conquer the dominant culture in land of promise.

3. Flirting With the Enemy

If we fast-forward for a brief visit to the New Testament Church, do Christians need to learn warfare tactics? Is it that important for a person to know how to fight against the enemy?" Yes, it is important. The Reformed church in the early stages of the Protestant reformation spoke and taught openly about the church militant.

The church militant is the church on earth that engages the enemies of the church. The 17th century theologian, Francis Turretin, aptly describes the difference between the church militant on earth and the church triumphant in heaven.

> The church militant suffers and struggles on earth; the church triumphant reigns and triumphs in heaven. The church militant is gathered by the ministry of the word and little by little advanced. The church militant is here hampered by many difficulties and infirmities. The church triumphant is glorious without spot or wrinkle" (*Institutes of Elenctic Theology*, by Francis Turretin, vol. 3, p. 633).

If there is an enemy and the enemy attacks, then fighting must follow. That the devil is our enemy is clear from Scripture. When Jesus explained the parable of the tares He said, "The enemy who sowed them is the devil" (Matthew 13:24-28). Christians have an enemy and his name is Satan. His angels are enemies. Christians would do well to remember the words of Jesus that were spoken to religious leaders of His day.

> Why do you not understand My speech? Because you are not able to listen to My word. You are of your father the devil, and the desires of your father you want to do. He was a murderer from the beginning, and does not stand in the truth, because there is no

truth in him. When he speaks a lie, he speaks from his own resources, for he is a liar and the father of it. (John 8:43-44)

A principle, lost in the age of false love, is that all human beings have a spiritual father, either God or Satan. Now to unleash the truth. Satan and his entourage translate to real enemies while God's people reside on this earth.

Othniel was the Judge in Israel when there was a whole generation of God's people born in the land that God had given His people. Unfortunately, they did not know how to fight against the enemies, namely the Philistines, the Canaanites, the Sardinians, and Hivites. Those ungodly tribes grew up in a dominant culture that was contrary to God's culture.

I fear that is the case today. Several generations have not been taught to protect themselves and their families from an ungodly culture. Our political ancestors were filled with biblical wisdom, and I grant that many of them were deists. However, they understood enough of the biblical teaching on this subject to establish the second amendment to the constitution. The amendment states that the people have a right to keep and bear arms. It gives the people a right to protect themselves. This principle applies to Christians. They must protect themselves from the evil forces that move with subliminal intent to deceive and destroy that which is true and godly. Warfare is a reality and it is a principle that applies to civil, secular, and spiritual life.

The church ignored the enemy and "served their gods." Truth and righteousness is now intermingled with deceit and ungodliness. The church at the beginning of the 21st century says very little about Satan and his large army. The doctrine of demonology has been grossly distorted by many evangelical preachers and teachers. Satan and his followers will try to persuade God's people that idolatry is not very bad. The old devil may try to convince pastors and church leaders that a little idolatry is good for church growth. For instance, Christians refer to buildings in terms of the church. Unbiblical traditions may promote church growth, but they are contrary to the Word of God. False doctrine is idolatrous.

The Bible often speaks of nations as being the enemies of God. The prophet Isaiah describes the enemies of God, as "the multitude of all the nations shall be, who fight against Mount Zion" (Isaiah 29:8). If Christians do not understand they have enemies, they will become comfortable with their enemies. It is dangerous for Christians to believe they do not have enemies. If Christians do not understand the dangers, it may bring suffering and affliction. However, to be comfortable with your enemy will bring devastation.

It appears that God's people found pleasure in their association with the enemies of God. The people of God married the enemy. Then they joined in worship with the enemy. God had already told His people, "You shall make no covenant with the inhabitants of this land" (Judges 2:2). The principle is manifest and universal. The bad will corrupt the good. A rotten apple lying next to a good apple will corrupt the good and then there will be two rotten apples. Some churches have flirted with the enemy and turned away from the good culture God gave them.

Flirting with the enemy will lead to apostasy and then comes affliction.

> So the children of Israel did evil in the sight of the LORD. They forgot the LORD their God, and served the Baals and Asherahs. Therefore the anger of the LORD was hot against Israel, and He sold them into the hand of Cushan-Rishathaim king of Mesopotamia; and the children of Israel served Cushan-Rishathaim eight years. (Judges 3:7-8)

The word "served" literally refers to slavery. Slavery is an inevitable institution. God's people in the Old Testament church understood the institution because they earned the opportunity to serve as slaves on various occasions. God commissioned Cushan-Rishathaim, the king of Mesopotamia, to enslave the Israelites during the period of the Judges. Why would God put His own people into slavery? Since slavery is an important biblical doctrine, a brief study is necessary.

Slavery is usually compared to freedom, which is a mistake. The words "freedom" and "slavery" signify two concepts that have been slaughtered by the ignorant, the anti-intellectuals, and the liberal American agenda. In the interest of sanity, it is time to re-examine freedom and slavery. In ancient Greece the word freedom implied one was not under restraint. Freedom, in its primitive form, referred to political and social freedom. The developed concept of freedom found in enlightenment terms refers to the self-determination of rational beings. Either definition opens the floodgate for autonomous individualism. The desires of the individual to judge, criticize, and express his or her individuality represents freedom of human fulfillment in a secular sense. Therefore, the individual thinks his or her freedom should be absolute.

Unfortunately the concept of freedom is obscure and delusive in the postmodern world of individual tyranny. The apex of distorted thinking about freedom is always absent of God's rule. For instance, John Locke said, "The natural liberty of man is to be free from any superior power on earth, and not to be under the will of legislative authority of man, but to have only the law of nature for his rule" (*Second Treatise of Government*). Today, freedom is often associated with John Locke's self-determination on one hand and immunity from responsibilities on the other.

The ideal for understanding freedom is God's idea of freedom. God "does whatever He pleases" (Psalm 115:3).

The ideal is further explained by an Old Testament scholar: "God is…supramundane in nature and life, and the absolutely unlimited One, who is able to do all things with a freedom that is conditioned only by Himself" (*Commentary on the Psalms*, by Keil and Delitzsch, vol. 2, p. 211). Human beings cannot do whatever they please because they act according to their sinful nature. Therefore his or her freedom cannot be absolute. If there is no absolute freedom, then human beings must, in some sense, be slaves and the slave will serve His master.

The Greek word for slave is *doulos,* which signified ownership. The slave belonged to someone else. For instance in Paul's letter to the Romans he declared himself to be "a slave of Christ Jesus" (Romans 1:1). The New Kings James Version and New American Standard Bible state that Paul was a bondservant of Jesus Christ. The Greek word translated bondservant is the Greek word *doulos.* Other translations use the word servant.

Today we think of a servant as one who is paid to carry out the mundane choirs of life. We hire such a one to cook, clean the house, cut the yard, etc. The Bible had a name for the hired servant. The Greek word that describes the hired hand is *misthotos.* The Bible describes the calling of James the son of Zebedee and John his brother who were mending fish nets in these terms: "And immediately He (Jesus) called them: and they left their father Zebedee in the boat with the hired servants (*misthotos*) and went away to follow Him. Paul did not consider himself a hired servant of Jesus Christ.

There is another word used in the text of some Greek manuscripts that describe a servant and that word is *therapon.* This word describes one who performs a service in the interest of public good. For instance Hebrews 3:5 refers to this word. "Now Moses was faithful in all His house as a servant (*therapon*) for a testimony of those things which would be spoken afterward... ." Paul was not just a public servant for the good of mankind.

There is another word used in the Greek text that describes a servant. The word is *huperetes*. This word describes one person who is subordinate to another person. Although Paul used this word to describe himself as a servant of Christ, the word is used most often to refer to officers acting submissively to their commander.

There is another word translated "servant" in the New Testament from the Greek word *diakovos*. It is translated into English as "deacon" but it is also translated "servant" such as when Paul describes Epaphras (Colossians 1:7). The idea is that Epaphras served in the church as a deacon in a way similar to the way a deacon would serve in the church today.

All these words except *doulos* represent a master/servant relationship. There is nothing humiliating in any of these terms, but the word slave (*doulos*) is humiliating. The English words bondservant or servant in Paul's letter to the Romans takes away from the original Greek word, which is slave (*doulos*). Even though a slave may achieve a high position in life such as the very responsible position held by Nehemiah or Daniel, the high position did not remove the stigma of slavery.

Paul was a Hebrew of Hebrews and a Roman Citizen. He held dual citizenship (actually triple citizenship when we consider his citizenship in heaven). A man who held his honored civil position would never have submitted himself as a slave to another human being. However, Paul was happy to be called a slave of Jesus Christ and calls himself a slave again in Philippians 1:1. Paul was happy to be called a slave to the one whom not only created him, but who redeemed him from his fallen estate and governed every action in Paul's life.

Truly it may be said that when one is a slave of Jesus Christ, that one has the truest liberty and the highest dignity. To be a slave brings with it a sense of belonging - a sense of ownership.   The kind of freedom sinful man seeks is an independent spirit.   Sinful man says, "I want to be my own self.   I want to control my own life.   I reject the institution of slavery."

Christians have different gifts and abilities, which should be nurtured, but too often forget that those are gifts and not self-achievements.   If we could see ourselves like the apostle Paul saw himself, we would desire to be called a slave of Jesus Christ.

There is a story told about a slave who despised the thought of being owned by an Englishman.   The slave said he would never obey so unworthy a master.   However after the purchase the slave learned that his new master had purchased him to give him his freedom.   The poor slave was so over-whelmed by joy and gratitude, he said, "I am your slave for ever."   His freedom made him a slave.

The Psalmist said it well when he said, "O Lord, truly I am Your servant; I am Your servant, the son of Your maidservant, You have loosed my bonds.   I will offer to You the sacrifice of thanksgiving and will call upon the name of the Lord."   (Psalm 116:16ff)

Now put yourself in the place of the Roman Christians who received Paul's letter.   Rome was a cosmopolitan city that was about as wicked a place to live as any you could image today.   Edward Gibbon in his monumental *History of the Decline and Fall of the Roman Empire* has estimated that "slaves under the reign of Claudius" reached nearly one-half of the population.   Others estimate that there were three slaves to every freeman.   It has been said that the slaves were worse off than animals during the day in which Paul wrote his letter to the Romans.   In Taylor's words on Civil Law he said:

> Slaves had no head of the state, no name, no title, or register; they were not capable to being injured; they had no heirs and therefore could make no will;   they

were not entitled to the rights and considerations of matrimony, and they had no relief in case of adultery; they could be sold, transferred, or pawned, as goods or personal estate; they might be tortured for evidence, punished at the discretion of their lord, and even put to death by his authority." (*History of the Christian Church*, by Philip Schaff, p. 447).

Now that you have a little history to think about, I ask you to put yourself in the place of those Roman Christians who received Paul's letter. How would you feel or think after reading the first line, "Paul a slave of Jesus Christ"? Did they ask the question "Is Paul crazy?" Who wants to be a slave? The answer is simple if we use God's definition for freedom and slavery. No one wants to be a slave unless the institution functions according to God's law. But, under God's law slavery is not a bad institution at all, if fact, if perfected it appears that Paul prefers biblical slavery over against secular freedom.

In his opening words to the Romans we find that this slave was called to be an apostle. The noble call of an apostle however never preceded the real effectual call of God to bring Paul into a state of salvation. Paul properly understood his relationship to Christ in terms of freedom and slavery. "Do you not know that when you present yourselves to someone as slaves for obedience, you are slaves of the one whom you obey, either of sin resulting in death, or of obedience resulting in righteousness?" (Romans 6:16). Did Paul find freedom in slavery? The answer is a resounding yes!

Paul's parentage, birth, gifts, education and call was distinctively different that the other apostles. As I said earlier, Paul possessed dual citizenship. His rhetorical and writing skills were superior to the other apostles. His education was very different. Paul studied at the feet of the great Rabbi Gamiliel and then he studied for years after he was converted in preparation for the ministry. The other apostles had a short three-year preparation. Paul was not ignorant of his unique call for in 2 Corinthians 11:5 Paul under inspiration said, "For I consider that I am not at all inferior to the most eminent apostles." Apparently his position as a slave did not interfere with his high position as an apostle.

The primary work of the Apostle Paul was not church politics, not church growth strategy, not living a happy healthy and prosperous life, nor complaining about his bondage to Jesus Christ. His primary work was to be obedient to his Lord and Master, the Lord Jesus Christ.

If you belong to Jesus Christ, You've been called to be a faithful, truthful, and sincere witness for Christ. You need to enter into this service as a slave of Christ. You need to ask Christ to accept your feeble efforts. You need to ask Christ to prepare you and teach you the whole counsel of God so you can obey all things that Christ has commanded, as any good slave would do if he loves his master. One of the best ways to make Christ the Lord in your life is for you to assume the posture of a slave, serving a perfect master.

We now return to the question, "Why would God put His own people into slavery under the authority of an ungodly culture?" They would not listen to God, so He had to prove that service to Him (being a slave to God) and living according to His cultural standards were incomparable to slavery in the enemy's culture. "Nevertheless they will be his servants, that they may distinguish My service from the kingdoms of the nations" (2 Chronicles 12:8). God made His people serve the Egyptians so that His people might distinguish between being a slave to God and being a slave to the enemies of God.

The children of Israel served Cushan-Rishathaim for eight years. "When the children of Israel cried out to the LORD, the LORD raised up a deliverer for the children of

Israel, who delivered them: Othniel the son of Kenaz, Caleb's younger brother" (Judges 3:9). Turning away from the Lord and becoming a slave to an ungodly way of life may take years, or for a particular church it may take generations. It all begins with "I know what the Bible says, but..." and then eventually the individual or a particular church may be swept away into apostasy. We have all been on that road to a greater or lesser degree. It is never too late to cry out to the Lord for His saving grace.

4. Message From God

And the children of Israel again did evil in the sight of the LORD. So the LORD strengthened Eglon king of Moab against Israel, because they had done evil in the sight of the LORD. Then he gathered to himself the people of Ammon and Amalek, went and defeated Israel, and took possession of the City of Palms. So the children of Israel served Eglon king of Moab eighteen years. But when the children of Israel cried out to the LORD, the LORD raised up a deliverer for them: Ehud the son of Gera, the Benjamite, a left-handed man. By him the children of Israel sent tribute to Eglon king of Moab. Now Ehud made himself a dagger (it was double-edged and a cubit in length) and fastened it under his clothes on his right thigh. So he brought the tribute to Eglon king of Moab. (Now Eglon was a very fat man.) And when he had finished presenting the tribute, he sent away the people who had carried the tribute. But he himself turned back from the stone images that were at Gilgal, and said, "I have a secret message for you, O king." He said, "Keep silence!" And all who attended him went out from him. So Ehud came to him (now he was sitting upstairs in his cool private chamber). Then Ehud said, "I have a message from God for you." So he arose from his seat. Then Ehud reached with his left hand, took the dagger from his right thigh, and thrust it into his belly. Even the hilt went in after the blade, and the fat closed over the blade, for he did not draw the dagger out of his belly; and his entrails came out. Then Ehud went out through the porch and shut the doors of the upper room behind him and locked them.

Judges 3:12-23

Your mind produced some kind of image as you read the story of Eglon and Ehud. If we made a movie based on that story, it would probably be rated "R" or at least "PG-13." It is easy to capture the image, but it will require some work to capture the meaning of the story. Christians cannot give this text the fair interpretive treatment it deserves until they look at it from the eyes of God's people in ages past. For example, what would an Israelite have thought of this text around 1000 B. C. during the reign of David? "The children of Israel did evil in the sight of the Lord" was probably inconceivable to the mind of the Old Testament believer during David or Solomon's reign. Israel thought they had defeated all the enemies around her during the reign of David. The Israelites probably wondered why the people of God during the time of the Judges, "forgot the Lord their God and served the Baals and Asherahs" (Judges 3:7). They even intermarried with the Canaanites (Judges 3:6). The peace and prosperity during the reign of David along with all the religious activity would make it very difficult for the Old Testament church to see that they were one generation away from flirting with the enemy. They missed God's message to the Judges.

It sounds like the United States and the church. Everything is so wonderful. There is plenty of money. The church is growing day by day and many churches can now boast of tens of thousands of members. The church is very religious but she flirts with the enemy and refuses to receive the message from God.

How would the exiled Israelites in Babylon from 586 B. C. to 516 B.C. understand the message to the Judges. Surely they were unable to think in terms of peace. They would read these words from Judges, "And the land had rest for eighty years" and wonder if their culture could experience peace. How would God's people living around 30 A.D. understand the book of Judges? They would read the book of Judges and find, "The Lord raised up a deliverer" (savior). Even though they wanted a savior, could they think in those terms because their political, social, and religious lives were under the control of Rome? It was a culture in chaos.

When we attempt to interpret history, we always find it difficult to place ourselves in the cultural and historical circumstances that will ultimately help us interpret history. There is a difference between what we commonly call history and biblical history. A Dictionary definition of history may be summarized as, "a continuous methodical record of important public events." History may also be defined, "the interpreted record of past events taken from data collected from various resources."

Biblical history is different, regardless of what the liberal revisionist historians tell you. Biblical history is descriptive history or normative history. Descriptive history describes something that happened such as we find in the life of King David.

It happened in the spring of the year, at the time when kings go out to battle, that David sent Joab and his servants with him, and all Israel; and they destroyed the people of Ammon and besieged Rabbah. But David remained at Jerusalem. Then it happened one evening that David arose from his bed and walked on the roof of the king's house. And from the roof he saw a woman bathing, and the woman was very beautiful to behold. So David sent and inquired about the woman. And someone said, "Is this not Bathsheba, the daughter of Eliam, the wife of Uriah the Hittite?" Then David sent messengers, and took her; and she came to him, and he lay with her, for she was cleansed from her impurity; and she returned to her house. And the woman conceived; so she sent and told David, and said, "I am with child." Then David sent to Joab, saying, "Send me Uriah the Hittite." And Joab sent Uriah to David. When Uriah had come to him, David asked how Joab was doing, and how the people were doing, and how the war prospered. And David said to Uriah, "Go down to your house and wash your feet." So Uriah departed from the king's house, and a gift of food from the king followed him. But Uriah slept at the door of the king's house with all the servants of his lord, and did not go down to his house. So when they told David, saying, "Uriah did not go down to his house," David said to Uriah, "Did you not come from a journey? Why did you not go down to your house?" And Uriah said to David, "The ark and Israel and Judah are dwelling in tents, and my lord Joab and the servants of my lord are encamped in the open fields. Shall I then go to my house to eat and drink, and to lie with my wife? As you live, and as your soul lives, I will not do this thing." Then David said to Uriah, "Wait here today also, and tomorrow I will let you depart." So Uriah remained in Jerusalem that day and the next. Now when David called him, he ate and drank before him; and he made him drunk. And at evening he went out to lie on his bed with the servants of his lord, but he did not go down to his house. In the morning it happened that David wrote a letter to Joab and sent it by the hand of Uriah. And he wrote in the letter, saying, "Set Uriah in the forefront of the hottest battle, and retreat from him, that he may be struck down and die." So it was, while Joab besieged the city, that he assigned Uriah to a place where he knew there were valiant men. Then the men of the city came out and fought with Joab. And some of the people of the servants of David fell; and Uriah the Hittite died also. (2 Samuel 11:1-17)

This is the infallible record of a historical event. The Christian mind recognizes the sin of adultery and murder in this historical event. However, it is not normal for Christians to commit adultery and murder. It is descriptive, not normative.

Normative history describes something that is normal for the Christian within the historical context. For example, "Jesus said to him, Away with you Satan! For it is written, You shall worship the Lord your God, and Him only you shall serve" (Matthew 4:10). It is normal for Christians to worship and serve God.

Christians ought to be careful to consider the historical context if they expect to come to grips with the culture that God gave them. The historical context for the book of Judges is that God's people have settled in the land of promise, but they failed to keep God's covenant. God told His people, "you shall make no covenant with the inhabitants of the land" (Judges 2:2). God's people broke the covenant and they provoked the Lord to anger, a recurring theme throughout the book of Judges. Evil provokes the Lord to anger. Can you imagine how angry the Lord is with the state of our nation and especially with the church? The infallible descriptive and normative history during the period of the Judges ought to be read with great care. Simply put, what goes around comes around!

During the period of the Judges, God raised up a big fat pagan king to punish the Israelites. Observe that the pagans used the principle of confederation to accomplish their task of punishing Israel. The confederation consisted of Moab, Ammon, and Amelek. God used the Moab, Ammon, Amelek confederacy to punish His people, because God's people ignored the principle of monarchy.

The book of Judges may not answer all our questions, but it will help us understand how Christians should live during cultural chaos. It is a message from God to believers and unbelievers. The message to believers is that God will save His people. The message to unbelievers is not good. Just ask Ehud!

As with any book of the Bible, certain principles stand out more than others. In the book of Judges there are three principles that are unambiguously present. Although I mentioned these principles in previous chapters, I bring them to your attention again because they are basic principles found throughout Scripture. They are indigenous to the human race. Ignorance or abuse of these three principles will certainly cause moral and spiritual decline in the church and culture in which you live.

First principle: The civil dimension of life is best ordered by the principle of confederation. The word confederate means to associate, cooperate, or affiliate for a common purpose. People join in a league to work toward a common cause. I think there has been some confusion about the use of the word confederation in contemporary thought. Let me make it clear that when I use the word confederation, it has nothing to do with the Confederate States of America during the middle of the 19th century. The concept known as a confederacy is a principle that stabilizes culture. Every level and aspect of human society is best ordered by this principle which is stamped on every nickel, *E pluribus unum*, out of many one. Out of man's sinfulness and inclination to error, there is safety in numbers. When a man and woman make a marriage covenant with each other before God, they form a confederacy. The principle of confederacy is found everywhere in Scripture for the well being of God's people.

Second principle: The spiritual dimension is best ordered by the principle of monarchy. The word monarchy comes from the word monarch or king. God is the only infallible, absolute, and perfect King. All earthly kings tend to be sinful with an inclination to usurp the authority given to God alone. Even the best of earthly kings may gravitate toward tyranny and oppression, because of the sinful nature.

Third principle: The salvation of the church and the prosperity of the culture depends on the work of the Messiah, the Lord Jesus Christ. His saving grace affects the church as well as the culture. As Christians examine the concept of a

God-centered culture, they should keep these three fundamental principles in mind.

God never leaves His people in sin. There is salvation for God's people. The Word of God describes the historical account of God raising up a savior for His people. It describes the murder of king Eglon by Ehud the savior. It is not a very pleasant scene.

The Word of God uses crass language in the book of Judges to describe a covert mission to assassinate a world leader. Is this descriptive or normative history? First you take the Word of God exactly like it is written. Do no try to moralize Scripture. Ehud was not acting out vengeance or hatred. Ehud was not trying to overthrow the existing government because of his own idealism. Plain and simple, God raised Ehud up to save His people from tyranny and bondage. Secondly, do not try to allegorize Scripture unless it is allegory. Ehud's dagger was not the sword of the Spirit. Simply put, his dagger was especially made to kill people.

The greatest abuse today is to try to use psychology to interpret Scripture. It would be easy to turn this into a dandy sermon with a title like, "Success in a left handed world." Abusing the Word of God will not help God's people. It is the Word of God and it is mixed with descriptive and normative history. It describes evil (see vs. 12 above). Even so, it gives the normal way in which God punishes His children (see vs. 12 above), if they forget the Lord.

Biblical history is different than unbiblical history, because biblical history is essentially a message from God to His church. The biblical history in the book of Judges is a message about what God does when His people sin against Him over and over again until He is finally provoked to anger. We are living in an age when our priorities are reversed in the church, much like the days of the Judges. It seems as if when God says "do not do something" the majority of professing Christians do it in spite of all the warnings from the Word of God. It seems as if when God says "do something" those same professing Christians do not do it in spite of all the warnings from the Word of God.

The message from God appears to fall on deaf ears and empty minds. The church on the broadest scale has become the scorn of the unbelieving world. Unfortunately, some of the professing conservative churches find it difficult to listen to the message from the Lord.

God also has a message for His enemies: Stop and think about the Moabite King named Eglon. He seems to have been a powerful ruler in that region having been instrumental in forming a successful confederacy. One must wonder how he thought of himself? I can only guess what he might have thought; I'm powerful, I'm the big man in this part of the world, people listen to me, I've traveled the world, I own lots of land and have plenty of money in the bank. The list rambles on endlessly, *ad nausiam.*

When unbelievers think too highly of themselves, they get a message from the Lord. However, they suppress it even though, "what may be known of God is manifest in them, for God has shown it to them" (Romans 1:19). At first unbelievers might think they want God's message, but when they hear the message it is not what they want. The message for unbelievers is that God will punish them for their sins even though it appears that God is prospering them. There is also the message of salvation if they believe and repent.

God sends messages to believers and unbelievers, sometimes by His hand of wrath in providence and other times He sends messages of grace and love by His Word. If you receive God's message and ignore it, remember that God will punish evil. (See Ezekiel 33:1-11 for a detailed account of this doctrine.) If you receive God's message and believe it and repent, remember that God delights in saving His people from their afflictions. Your enemy may test and tempt you, but remember it pleases God to give His people rest from their enemies in this life. There is the promise of eternal rest in the eternal Sabbath.

5. No Men in Israel

When Ehud was dead, the children of Israel again did evil in the sight of the LORD. So the LORD sold them into the hand of Jabin king of Canaan, who reigned in Hazor. The commander of his army was Sisera, who dwelt in Harosheth Hagoyim. And the children of Israel cried out to the LORD; for Jabin had nine hundred chariots of iron, and for twenty years he had harshly oppressed the children of Israel. Now Deborah, a prophetess, the wife of Lapidoth, was judging Israel at that time.

Judges 4:1-4

The history of the God's people during the period of the Judges ought to be studied in light of the contemporary western culture. Christians ought to study the Judges because the cycles of history are amazingly predictable. The cycles are evident, not only in the book of Judges, but also in the history of the church.

2:11 - Then the Children of Israel did evil in the sight of the Lord and served the Baals.

2:20 - The anger of the Lord was hot against Israel.

3:9 – Lord raised up a deliverer, a man named Othniel.

3:11 – The land had rest for forty years.

3:7 - The children of Israel did evil in the sight of the Lord.

3:12 - The children of Israel again did evil in the sight of the Lord.

3:15 – The Lord raised up a deliverer, a man named Ehud.

3:30 – The land had rest for eighty years.

4:1 - When Ehud was dead the children of Israel again did evil in the sight of the Lord.

4:4 – Now Deborah, a prophetess, the wife of Lapi-doth, was judging Israel at the time.

The above outline covers about ninety years of history. The few words that describe so much history of the Hebrew culture are a mere generalization of the way of life for the Old Testament church during the period of the Judges.

A better summary for the period of the Judges is found in the latter chapters (see chapters 17-21). Four times in chapters 17-21 we are told that, "In those days there was no king in Israel; everyone did what was right in his own eyes." It is a general statement that describes the culture of the Israelites and the dominant worldview commonly known as individualism during the period of the Judges.

The United States is in a similar state of affairs at the beginning of the third millennium. With the absence of any respect for the law of God and the unconcern for a standard of truth, we see the violation of two very important concepts. Rather than acting in a lawful confederacy for the stability of the culture, "everyone does what is right in his own eyes." Rather than acting with respect toward the absolute cosmic monarch, "everyone does what is right in his own eyes."

This is the prevalent attitude in this country and especially in Protestant churches. Christians would do well to remember that all human beings are born under authority. They are not born free. They do not have a license to do anything they want to do. No man is free from the law of God, because as the Bible says, the law of God is written in their hearts and their conscience bearing witness of all men (Romans 2:14-15). No man is free from the laws of intelligent human discourse. Yet it seems that the majority of our society ignores the law of God and intelligent human discourse. They worship the god of relativism. "Everyone does what is right in his own eyes." The Lord is provoked to anger when His people disregard the principles in His Word and adopt individualism as their god. When the Lord is angry, people may as well expect to see his anger. God expressed His anger to the Israelites by selling the Israelites into slavery. For twenty years, King Jabin, the Canaanite King, was the instrument of wrath that God used to punish the Israelites (Judges 4:3). The Bible states the children of Israel were harshly oppressed. During this oppression and suffering you would think that God would raise up a deliverer or a savior for the people. God raised up two deliverers, Othniel (Judges 3:9) and Ehud (Judges 3:15). When Ehud died the people of Israel, "did evil in the sight of the Lord."

Even though God's children were "harshly oppressed," the Bible does not mention their plea for help or that God raised up a deliverer. The Bible does not say that God raised Deborah to Judge Israel, it simply says, "Now Deborah, a prophetess, the wife of Lapidoth, was judging Israel at that time" (Judges 4:4). The nation of Israel found itself without a man as a Judge. The nation of Israel was uniquely a church/state ruled by God's appointed servants. The assertion that there were no men in Israel does not mean that some male human beings did not reside there, but the Bible makes it clear there was no male leadership in the church or the state.

There is a simple question that needs a simple answer. What is wrong with having a woman rule the church and the state? The answer is very simple. That is not the natural authority structure established by God. In the beginning, before sin entered into the world God said, "it is not good that man should be alone; I will make him a helper comparable to him" (Genesis 2:18). God created the woman to help the man fulfill the cultural mandate, not rule over man. The Fall of man into sin was a complex factor, because it involved the physical culture and the spiritual dimension. The cultural/spiritual punishment from God was manifest in the women overstepping the authority of her husband, "Your

47

desire shall be for your husband, And he shall rule over you" (Genesis 3:16).

Deborah was following her natural sinful instincts by assuming the role assigned to men. However, God used Deborah to accomplish his purpose, just as He uses whomever He pleases. In extraordinary circumstances, God may use a donkey to accomplish His purpose (Numbers 22:22ff). It is never wise to pray that God will use you; it is wise to pray that God will work in you His desire to serve Him. Then, you work it out to accomplish God's purpose in your life.

My opinion about Deborah's leadership is not important. However, the Word of God is important. What is the biblical doctrine relative to women doing what men ought to do, other than what I have already mentioned? The Bible teaches that one person has authority over another person by virtue of God's will on the matter. There are principles in Scripture that explain women leadership in the church and in the state. In the Old Testament, the church and the state were joined under one monarch, the Lord God almighty. He alone is able to instruct man infallibly for all of faith and life. I call it the principle of monarchy. A few Scriptural references should be sufficient to establish the principle of submission to authority.

> Eph. 5:23 – "The husband is head of the wife."
> Eph. 5:22 – "Wives, submit yourselves to your own husbands, as to the Lord."
> 1 Cor. 11:9 – Nor was man created for the woman, but woman for the man."
> 1 Tim 2:11ff – "Let a woman learn in silence with all submission. . .I do not permit a woman to teach or to have authority over a man, but to be in silence."

Christians ought not ignore the Bible.

Some preachers and teachers argue that Deborah is the perfect example to prove that God mandates female leadership both in the church and state. If that is true then the Bible has contradicted itself and cannot be trusted as the Word of God. Furthermore, the Book of Judges describes some of the lowest spiritual times for the people of God in the history of the Bible. The period of the Judges demonstrated ruthless and reckless leadership from men, who ought to have submitted to the authority of God. The Judges should never be presented as a model, since it is largely descriptive history, not normative history.

The men of Israel were not acting like men at all. Deborah assumed her role as the leader of the Old Testament state and church. The Bible indicates she was a prophetess. There is no evidence from the Word of God that God appointed her to that position, such as was the case with Aaron (Exodus 7:1) and Isaiah (Isaiah 6:9-13). Anyhow, she led the state (she was the Commander in chief) as well a spiritual leader.

A question that any serious Bible student may ask is, "why would God allow a woman to rule over men when He could have raised up a man just as easily?" I do not know. I can only speculate based on my understanding of the general teaching of Scripture. I believe it was so that the men would be humiliated and shamed for their lack of leadership.

The same problem exists in the church today. To a large degree men have abandoned their post. It is somewhat different in the modern church. Often the men will have the title, but the women actually make the decisions and do the work that men ought to do.

Apparently, the men of Israel did not have the courage to fight. Certain tribes refused to confederate for the purpose of waging war against the enemy (Judges 5:16-18). They ignored the principle of confederation. There was a limited confederation. Deborah summoned Barak to leadership. He refused to take a leadership position unless she would accompany him in battle. Deborah agreed but prophesied that the glory of victory would go to a woman. It was a woman, Jael the Kenite, who drove a tent peg through the head of General Sisera, the commander of the Canaanite army. (Judges 4:21)

The men of Israel, like their father's before them, and like some Christians today, fail to follow the principle of monarchy. God is the cosmic King, the ruler over all men and women. His design was for an orderly culture with everyone fulfilling their respective places according to His design for order and harmony.

The source of a cultural milieu, often inherited from previous generations, needs to find a primary authority. If man is the authority, the culture will end in chaos. If God is the authority, the culture will continue with civil, social and spiritual harmony and order.

The Lord God has given the church His law. It encompasses the whole counsel of God. It teaches the need to depend on the mercy of God. First, it is God's mercy that saves His people from the condemnation of the law and secondly, it is God's mercy that allows them to obey the gospel. May God have mercy on His church and may the elect of God obey the gospel for salvation.

When God's people obey the gospel, godly men and women will capture the culture with their words and works. They will engage the culture with winsome personalities and wise directions for leading His church into the eternal Sabbath.

6. Chasing New gods

In the days of Shamgar, son of Anath, in the days of Jael, the highways were deserted, and the travelers walked along the byways. Village life ceased, it ceased in Israel, until I, Deborah, arose, arose a mother in Israel. They chose new gods; Then there was war in the gates; Not a shield or spear was seen among forty thousand in Israel. My heart is with the rulers of Israel who offered themselves willingly with the people. Bless the Lord!

Judges 5:6-9

Religious and civil life in the United States of America appears to be very similar to the biblical descriptive history during the period of the Judges. Religious worship was suited to what every man thought was right in his own eyes. Civil life was in a state of confusion because the nation failed in its understanding of the principle of confederation and the principle of monarchy. A culture consists of people who have some connection to the secular and the sacred, the church and the state. God's people must be the instruments of reformation, first in the church and then in the state. Jonathan Edwards summarized his understanding of the church/state relationship.

> The civil authorities having nothing to do with matters ecclesiastical, with those things which relate to conscience and eternal salvation or with any matter religious as religious, is reconcilable still with their having to do with some matters that, in some sense, concern religion. For although they have to do with nothing but civil affairs, and although their business extends no further than the civil interests of the people, yet by reason of the profession of religion. . . many things become civil which otherwise would

not... Thus it is for the civil interest of a people not to be disturbed in their public assembling for divine worship, that is, it is for the general peace, profit, and pleasure of 'em in this world. (*Rational Biblical Theology of Jonathan Edwards*, vol. 3, p. 418)

However, if the church has no interest in civil life, then the church has no interest in obeying all that Christ has commanded. Jesus said that God's people are the "the salt of the earth and the Light of the world." The public square does not exclude ethics. If we pretend that the law of God is outdated, we make mockery of God and His inspired Word, for Jesus said, "Whoever, therefore breaks one of the least of these commandments, and teaches men so, shall be called least in the kingdom of heaven" (Matthew 5:19). God's people cannot be the instruments of God's graceful gospel, unless they embrace the full counsel of God and reject false religion. If they embrace the full counsel of God and reject false religion, they must be interested in the civil affairs of our society.

The culture in Israel during the period of the Judges reminds me of any city in this country at the beginning of the 21st century. "The highways were deserted, and the travelers walked along the byways" (Judges 5:6). The conditions in Israel were such that travel was disrupted because of the robbers that roamed the land. Village life ceased in Israel (Judges 5:7). There was a disruption of normal life. Shops were closed, crops had to be abandoned, and there was a general economic depression, because small villages were unprotected from the ravaging Canaanites. This is a description of the state/church in Israel during the period of the Judges; it is similar to our present state of cultural chaos in this country. The chaos, confusion, and apostasy in Israel was not the people merely disobeying the rules, it was the dismissal of fundamental principles. Any culture especially a culture influenced by Christians, whether it is to a greater or lesser degree a Christian culture, must have one God that is the supreme monarch.

The devolution of ungodly principles from previous generations creates skepticism in the culture. For that reason, the Israelite culture "chose new gods." The Old Testament church, as well as the church in the New Testament, inclines itself to chase new gods. Idolatry is her name and she is the mother of all sins. It was idolatry that provoked God to punish His people and to put His people into a state of slavery.

Eve was deceived to idolize herself, rather than worship the true and living God. As a result of her idolatry, God's wrath was provoked and the punishment for that sin will be eternally remembered. The sin of idolatry lies at the heart of all human rebellion. Idolatry is the primary way in which men and women reject the sovereignty of God.

God has spoken to His children in Holy Scripture about how they are to relate to every aspect of life, career, possessions, family, friends, entertainment, politics and the list is endless. Yet, when I say, "the Bible says" the response I often get is, "that's your opinion."

The idolater is the independent god maker. The idolater says, "it is my way or no way." The idolater refuses to listen to the Word of God. The idolater is the one who brings the judgment of God to the church, throwing the culture into further chaos.

I wish semantic categories were not necessary in the science of interpretation, but because of our sinful estate, we cannot think in ultimate and absolute terms. We tend to place conditions to ultimate and absolute propositions. If we think in those categories, we change the ultimate to the proximate and the absolute to the conditional. If it takes a minute to digest this principle, it will be worth it. Now, let us apply the principle. The ultimate and absolute is the one true and living

God. The proximate and conditional is the world of false gods. It is either one or the other and they cannot be mixed.

The life of any culture requires an object of worship. Life becomes lifeless without worship. In the life of a culture, idolatry becomes a way of life. It comes in the shape of a worldview. It may be the idolatry of prosperity, the idolatry of power, or the idolatry of nationalism or it may be a personal or collective idol. The monarchial principle may be ignored, but there will be consequences.

> When you beget children and grandchildren and have grown old in the land and act corruptly and make a carved image in the form of anything, and do evil in the sight of the LORD your God to provoke Him to anger, I call heaven and earth to witness against you this day, that you will soon utterly perish from the land which you cross over the Jordan to possess; you will not prolong your days in it, but will be utterly destroyed. And the LORD will scatter you among the peoples, and you will be left few in number among the nations where the LORD will drive you. (Deuteronomy 4:25-27)

The dangers of idolatry are destructive. It hurts the sinner, adversely affects the culture, and grieves God. The idolater must acknowledge his or her idolatry, believe God, and repent or perish. The wickedness that so easily accompanies idolatry must be removed or otherwise God will visit with His hand of wrath. There can be no peace when God's punishment for wickedness visits the church or the culture. "There is no peace," says the Lord, "for the wicked" (Isaiah 48:22).

The church ought to be engaged in the culture by rejecting the false religion derived from idolatry and be a useful instrument for religious reform. Chasing new gods will lead to the fatal association with the enemy. The unhealthy relationship with the enemies of God, will always take you into the enemy camp.

It is a great mistake to believe that God does not have enemies. You can be assured that if God has enemies, then God's people also have enemies. It is for that very reason that the Bible has an abundance of imprecatory prayers, such as the one we find in Deborah's poem. "Thus let all Your enemies perish, O Lord" (Judges 5:31). A definition of imprecatory prayers will be useful at this point.

> Those Psalms which most clearly call upon God's judgment to prevail over His enemies. The church has not only argued over whether we can pray such prayers, but has struggled with how to understand these in the context of the grace of God, and His command that we love our enemies. These difficulties are greatly alleviated if we understand these words as coming from the mouth of Christ, who in His innocence, can and does judge the guilty. In Him, and for His glory we may likewise pray them. (*Theological Terms in Layman Language*, by Martin Murphy, p. 69)

Without studying the full counsel of God, the words "let all Your enemies perish" may lead someone to think that it is an isolated reference in Scripture. The following is a representative sample of imprecatory Psalms taken from the Word of God.

> Psalm 35:26 - Let them be ashamed and brought to mutual confusion who rejoice at my hurt.

> Psalm 40:14 - Let them be ashamed and brought to mutual confusion who seek to destroy my life.

Psalm 70:2 - Let them be ashamed and confounded who seek my life.

Psalm 97:7 - Let them be put to shame who serve carved images, who boast of idols.

Jeremiah 17:18 - Let them be ashamed who persecute me and do not let me be put to shame.

An imprecatory prayer, such as the one found in Deborah's poem is a legitimate prayer for justice. It is not a prayer of hatred and bitterness but a prayer to vindicate the honor, character, and essence of God. The English Baptist pastor, Charles Spurgeon, said, "God's people may well look with derision upon their enemies since they are the objects of divine contempt. They scoff at us, but we may with far greater reason laugh them to scorn, because the Lord our God considers them as less than nothing and vanity."

If you lived in the 16th century Europe, or the 21st century in the United States (actually un-united), or the 25th century in this world, God will have enemies. Therefore, the true church will have enemies and individual Christians will have enemies. The culture will be divided, but the church ought to be united. Unfortunately, that is not the case. For example, there were four tribes among the Israelites (Gilead representing Gad and the half tribe of Manasseh, Dan, and Asher) who did not heed the call to action against the enemies of God (Judges 5:17). They failed to follow the principle of confederation for the well-being of their culture. The immediate context does not explain why these tribes failed to confederate with the other tribes to fight against the enemy. I will suggest two possible reasons based on my understanding of the history of the Old and New Testament church. Maybe they were satisfied because the enemy did not assault them. Maybe they enjoyed the close relationship they had with the enemy. Maybe the sensual pleasure derived from false worship with the enemy was irresistible. False doctrine leads to false worship and without repentance ends with a false relationship with the true God.

False doctrine found its way into many Protestant churches over the past couple of hundred years, because many church leaders did not see the error in false doctrine or were either afraid to speak against the error. For example, some dispensational theologians are antinomian; they do not teach the necessity of keeping the Law of God. This false doctrine quickly infects the doctrine of sanctification. Several prominent evangelical theologians have denied the literal existence of Hell. This false doctrine questions the authority of Scripture and the doctrine of salvation. The assault against preaching and teaching God's truth was unimportant to many in the church, because programs, buildings, and other culturally accommodating ideas were more important than working to leave sound doctrine for generations to come. The ways of the world were readily adopted into worship and practice. Preaching the Word of God has been labeled as "hate speech." The evils of the success syndrome, the health and wealth gospel and the ten best ways to grow a church, found a place in many if not most evangelical churches. The people of God have acted just like Gilead, Dan, and Asher. They stayed "beyond the Jordan" and "sat in their sheepfolds" and failed to lift a hand against the enemy of God. The tribes of Ephraim, Benjamin, Zebulun, Issachar and Naphtali were the instruments of God on earth to fight the enemy (Judges 5:14-18). These tribes entered "the valley" and fought for the land God had promised to them. It was that godly confederacy that brought rest to the land for 40 yrs.

There is a raging battle today, in the church and in the culture. Chasing new gods is the thrill in the modern American 21st century culture. A popular greeting at the beginning of the 21st century in America is, "I am good."

With the cultural mess, the syncretism of true and false worship, and the banishment of rational thought, we ought to ask, "who is good?" The silly notion that a person is good must mean the culture is good. The Bible has the answer to the question, "who is good?" "No one is good but One, that is, God" (Mark 10:18). "The heart is deceitful above all things, and desperately wicked" (Jeremiah 17:9). "For the wrath of God is revealed from heaven against all ungodliness and unrighteousness of men, who suppress the truth in unrighteousness..." (Romans 1:18).

The church will have its affect on the culture when she learns to resist the wicked idolatry and recognize the wicked enemy who has crept into her assembly. It is time to take the offense, get on the playing field, pick up the shield and spear, seek the blessing of God, and go to spiritual war against the wickedness of the ungodly culture that seeks to take over the church by the charm of chasing new gods.

7. Fakes Are Failures

*Now it came to pass the same night that the LORD said to him,
"Take your father's young bull, the second bull of seven years old,
and tear down the altar of Baal that your father has, and cut down
the wooden image that is beside it; and build an altar to the LORD
your God on top of this rock in the proper arrangement, and take
the second bull and offer a burnt sacrifice with the wood of the
image which you shall cut down." So Gideon took ten men from
among his servants and did as the LORD had said to him. But
because he feared his father's household and the men of the city
too much to do it by day, he did it by night. And when the men of
the city arose early in the morning, there was the altar of Baal, torn
down; and the wooden image that was beside it was cut down, and
the second bull was being offered on the altar which had been built.
So they said to one another, "Who has done this thing?" And when
they had inquired and asked, they said, "Gideon the son of Joash
has done this thing." Then the men of the city said to Joash,
"Bring out your son, that he may die, because he has torn down the
altar of Baal, and because he has cut down the wooden image that
was beside it." But Joash said to all who stood against him,
"Would you plead for Baal? Would you save him? Let the one
who would plead for him be put to death by morning! If he is a
god, let him plead for himself, because his altar has been torn
down!" Therefore on that day he called him Jerubbaal, saying,
"Let Baal plead against him, because he has torn down his altar."*

Judges 6:25-40

People are very religious and some people are seriously and passionately committed to their religious beliefs. How
many times have I heard the expression: "I just don't talk
religion with my neighbors." Maybe they are afraid a discussion about religion might offend their neighbor. Then there
are others who although very religious, they are unconcerned
and perhaps even ashamed of their religion. In either case, it
is the understanding or misunderstanding of the nature and

character of their god or their gods that make them that way. People have a desire for religious activity, but their lack of understanding and assurance cause them to keep their god or gods to themselves.

It is common for unconverted sinful man to hide the nature and character of his god. To camouflage the true character of his god, it is replaced with an image that is more palatable to the public sector. For instance, a person may hide the god of greed and covetousness with the god of financial success. Outwardly, he worships financial success, but inwardly it is greed and covetousness. A person may hide the god of hatred with the god of gossip and slander. Then there are those who hide worship abuse behind church attendance on Sunday. There are many ways to hide the nature and character of a god with what appears legitimate according to the standards of the world. False gods are fake gods. They may appear to be real, but they do not exist in the metaphysical world in a favorable relationship with God. They do not exist in eternity.

The true and living God commanded the Israelites to tear down the altars of the false gods. However, the Old Testament Church did not listen to God. The temptation to turn away from the true God to worship other gods is often encouraged by religious leaders, family and public influence from the culture. Religious leaders may use their position to encourage people to follow false gods. Every believer in every age of the church ought to pay close attention to God's warnings. Would a true prophet of God encourage God's people to violate the first commandment and follow false gods? The Word of God has an answer.

> If there arises among you a prophet or a dreamer of dreams, and he gives you a sign or a wonder, and the sign or the wonder comes to pass, of which he spoke to you, saying, 'Let us go after other gods'—which

you have not known—'and let us serve them,' you shall not listen to the words of that prophet or that dreamer of dreams, for the LORD your God is testing you to know whether you love the LORD your God with all your heart and with all your soul. You shall walk after the LORD your God and fear Him, and keep His commandments and obey His voice; you shall serve Him and hold fast to Him. But that prophet or that dreamer of dreams shall be put to death, because he has spoken in order to turn you away from the LORD your God, who brought you out of the land of Egypt and redeemed you from the house of bondage, to entice you from the way in which the LORD your God commanded you to walk. So you shall put away the evil from your midst. (Deuteronomy 13:1-5)

Unfortunately, family and friends will tempt Christians to follow false gods. The Bible warns Christians relative to the danger of being persuaded to follow false gods.

If your brother, the son of your mother, your son or your daughter, the wife of your bosom, or your friend who is as your own soul, secretly entices you, saying, 'Let us go and serve other gods,' which you have not known, neither you nor your fathers, of the gods of the people which are all around you, near to you or far off from you, from one end of the earth to the other end of the earth, you shall not consent to him or listen to him, nor shall your eye pity him, nor shall you spare him or conceal him; but you shall surely kill him; your hand shall be first against him to put him to death, and afterward the hand of all the people. And you shall stone him with stones until he dies, because he sought to entice you away from the LORD your

God, who brought you out of the land of Egypt, from
the house of bondage. (Deuteronomy 13:6-10)

Another source of temptation to follow false gods may be the
culture in which you live.

If you hear someone in one of your cities, which the
LORD your God gives you to dwell in, saying,
'Corrupt men have gone out from among you and
enticed the inhabitants of their city, saying, "Let us go
and serve other gods'"—which you have not
known— then you shall inquire, search out, and ask
diligently. And if it is indeed true and certain that
such an abomination was committed among you, you
shall surely strike the inhabitants of that city with the
edge of the sword, utterly destroying it, all that is in it
and its livestock—with the edge of the sword.
(Deuteronomy 13:12-15)

The first objection one may have against the text in
Deuteronomy is "we do not live in a theocracy; therefore, the
judicial case law requiring death does not apply in the New
Testament church." A sensible, intelligent Christian will not
look for objections to the Word of God, but rather will look
for the eternal principles. In the words of Dr. J. Gresham
Machen, "a nation that tramples thus upon the law of God,
that tramples upon the basic principles of integrity, is headed
for destruction unless it repents in time" (*Education,
Christianity, and the State*, by Dr. J Gresham Machen, p.
141). The church provokes the Lord to anger with their false
worship. The civil culture, which includes the state, provokes
the Lord to anger by ignoring natural law and the evidence of
God's presence so clearly seen in the light of nature. The
church continues to ignore the monarchical principle and the
state continues to ignore the principle of confederation. The

monarchial principle places God on His throne. The confederation principle bonds together like-minded believers.

If the culture persuades the church to worship false gods, she will become enslaved to the wickedness of false worship. Once the culture controls worship, professing Christians will easily be persuaded to adopt an ungodly way of life.

During the period of the Judges God's people were taken into slavery by the worshippers of false gods. Then the Israelites would beg God for mercy; literally, the Bible says, "the children of Israel cried out to the Lord." God used the men and women to deliver His people from bondage.

These godly men and a woman followed two fundamental principles that delivered the Israelites from being enslaved by the enemy, one enemy being inward and the other being outward.

1. They confederated the tribes of Israel for warfare.

2. They turned to the King of kings for the Word of God.

Gideon was a man that understood both of these principles. They gave him confidence and assurance because he understood the reality of the presence of the enemy. Gideon had to face two enemies. The first one the Bible describes as, "all the Midianites and the Amalekites, the people of the East, gathered together; and they crossed over and encamped in the Valley of Jezreel" (Judges 6:33). Unfortunately, Gideon had another enemy, a very subtle enemy, and an enemy that most people would not call an enemy. The other enemy was Gideon's father. Gideon's father was a Baal worshipper. The Lord spoke to Gideon saying, "Take your father's young bull, the second bull of seven years old, and tear down the altar of Baal that your father has, and cut down the wooden image…"

(Judges 6:25). Gideon's father worshipped false gods. The culture around Gideon worshipped false gods. Those who worship false gods are not your friends.

When idolatry, anti-biblical worship, and a general disdain for the Word of God prevails, the church becomes the object of scorn, mistrust and abandonment. The church becomes venerable to cultural subjugation. It is then that the individual Christian must persevere and become a Gideon. God instructed Gideon to tear down the altar of Baal, an altar that belonged to Gideon's earthly father.

The liberal theologian and the modern thinker might say, "Surely God would not break up a family over a religious dispute." God does not break up families. Families break up families. God does demand truthfulness in worship and obedience to His law. Earthly familial responsibilities do not truncate spiritual responsibilities to God the Father. Jesus said, "Do not think that I came to bring peace on earth. I did not come to bring peace but a sword….He who loves father or mother more than Me is not worthy of Me…" (Matthew 10:34-39). If Gideon expected to save the Old Testament church from oppression and suffering, he had to risk severing a relationship with his family. Gideon heeded God's call for action.

Gideon destroyed the altar of Baal, although not in the sight of all men. He had his servants destroy it at night. Gideon feared his father's household. God called Gideon to be obedient and faithful, not heroic in the sense of garnishing accolades from God or man. It is a lesson every Christian should learn. There is a hymn that speaks eloquently to this call from God to confront the irreligious culture, "trust and obey because there is no other way…"

Gideon did find himself standing squarely against the enemy. The destruction of the altar of Baal provoked the enemy to put Gideon to death, even though Gideon did the right thing. It is unbelievable; the death sentence for destroying a silly altar. Religious worship stirs the passions of rational creatures. Gideon's father, his earthly father, the one who presumably worshipped Baal, apparently repented and would have understood the words of Jesus, "no one can serve two masters."

The altar of Baal and the altar of the true and living God could not stand side by side. Remember when Elijah was on Mt. Carmel and Ahab had sent for the children of Israel and the prophets. Elijah said, "How long will you falter between two opinions? If the Lord is God follow him; but if Baal follow him." The false god was put to the test and failed. False gods will always fail. Fakes are failures.

Was Baal a fake god? Gideon's father said, "If he [Baal] is a god, let him plead for himself, because his altar has been torn down!" This was nothing more than a test to see if the false god had the power it claimed to have. The false god failed, because it was a fake god and fake gods are not real. Fake gods only have the appearance of reality. Fake gods are like mirages, they only appear to be real, but when you need them, they really do not exist.

Gideon's fleece is a good example of the true and living God, the God who will always pass the test.

> So Gideon said to God, "If You will save Israel by my hand as You have said look, I shall put a fleece of wool on the threshing floor; if there is dew on the fleece only, and it is dry on all the ground, then I shall know that You will save Israel by my hand, as You have said." And it was so. When he rose early the next morning and squeezed the fleece together, he wrung the dew out of the fleece, a bowlful of water. Then Gideon said to God, "Do not be angry with me, but let me speak just once more: Let me test, I pray, just once more with the fleece; let it now be dry only on the fleece, but on all the ground let there be dew."

And God did so that night. It was dry on the fleece only, but there was dew on all the ground. (Judges 6:36-40)

The symbolism of the fleece is noteworthy for Christians so they can compare the true God with the fake gods. God was able to show Gideon that the Old Testament church would be blessed, even though it appeared that the nations around the church were flourishing. Gideon needed assurance that the true and living God would save His people and His culture, but destroy the enemy culture.

Jesus Christ promises that His church will prevail. To prevail, it must engage in the culture with the eternal principles from the Word of God. If the church worships fake gods, she will provoke the anger of the Lord. Eventually the false gods will fail and Jesus Christ will ultimately stand. Christians, confederate against the enemy and trust the King of kings for salvation.

8. Staying Focused

Then the men of Israel said to Gideon, "Rule over us, both you and your son, and your grandson also; for you have delivered us from the hand of Midian." But Gideon said to them, "I will not rule over you, nor shall my son rule over you; the LORD shall rule over you." Then Gideon said to them, "I would like to make a request of you, that each of you would give me the earrings from his plunder." For they had golden earrings, because they were Ishmaelites. So they answered, "We will gladly give them." And they spread out a garment, and each man threw into it the earrings from his plunder. Now the weight of the gold earrings that he requested was one thousand seven hundred shekels of gold, besides the crescent ornaments, pendants, and purple robes which were on the kings of Midian, and besides the chains that were around their camels' necks. Then Gideon made it into an ephod and set it up in his city, Ophrah. And all Israel played the harlot with it there. It became a snare to Gideon and to his house.

Judges 8:22-27

Godly people must have the desire to live according to God's plan and God's will. God reveals His plan and His will to His people from His Word. In God's plan, He established the church and the state. God's will is that the church and the state co-exist in harmony with the Word of God.

God's plan and will include an understanding of the roles of the governing authorities particularly as they relate to Christians. For instance, the Bible says, "Let every person be in subjection to the governing authorities" (Romans 13:1). There are two ways to understand that verse. Some people interpret that verse with a universal positive, "Do everything the government says do." Others interpret it to mean that Christians should obey the government according to a Christian world and life view. If Christians are true to the text in Romans, they must stay focused on the Word of God.

The life of Gideon more than any of the other Judges is one of the most popular stories in Judges. The story of Gideon is found in many children's Bible stories. Gideon stayed focused on the true and living God, for a time, but eventually his attention turned to false gods and in the end, he fell into sin. Falling into some sin is common to all men. Sometimes people collectively fall into sin. A particular church or denomination may fall into sin. A nation that followed godly principles in its beginning may likewise fall into some special sin or many sins for that matter.

Israel did not keep her eyes on the true and living God. Israel was attracted to the false and dead gods of the nations around her. Just as Eve saw that the fruit was good, pleasant, and desirable, so the Israelites saw that the false gods were good pleasant and desirable.

Rather than consulting her husband, Eve's individualism prevailed. Remember that the husband and wife are, in some sense of the word, a confederacy. God brought them together so that they might become one. However, seeking her own way, Eve wanted to rule her own individual life. She acted is if she was a king with absolute power. Likewise, Israel as a state and a church acted independently of the Word of God. They deserved God's displeasure and punishment.

During the period of the Judges, God used the Midianites to punish Israel for her sins. However, God showed mercy to the Israelites and He used Gideon to deliver the Israelites from slavery. The punishment by the Midianites must have been severe. The Israelites had to live in caves in the mountains to escape the severe punishment. The Midianites raided the fields of the Israelites, stole their livestock and literally destroyed the land. The Bible says, "Israel was greatly impoverished because of the Midianites."

The history of western civilization reveals that the church has experienced an impoverished condition because of cultural invasion. At various times throughout western civilization, chaos has been a common expression of culture. The dilapidated state of our nation is the result of the church disregarding the authority of Scripture. The civil culture in the United States is in a state of chaos as I write this book at the beginning of the 21st century. Either evangelical churches in the United States have forgotten the principles of confederation and monarchy, or they simply choose to ignore them.

The causes of the turmoil in western culture and the bankruptcy of truth in the church are too many to enumerate. Without mentioning proper names and events, it has pleased God to use liberal politicians, theologians, elite managerial control on Wall Street, a therapeutic revolution and the rich aesthetes who have proclaimed that image is everything. God uses these people to punish His people to get the attention of the whole church.

Rather than acting in a confederation to fight the evils of abortion, injustice in the judicial system, or the philosophically bankrupt educational system, Christians wanted individual independence. "Every man did what was right in his own eyes." Well would it have been if professing Christians had identified the causes that lead to these evils and then ejected them from the church and culture.

The Lord spoke to the Israelites by prophets speaking the words of the Lord. Likewise, the Lord has given His Word, found in the Bible. Unfortunately, the church has not obeyed the voice of God. The culture ignores God's natural law written on the heart of every person. Christians must begin by returning to the Lord. If a professing Christian returns to the Lord, he or she must submit to God's Word.

According to His Word, He has given pastors to the minister to the church. The Bible explains the important role of a pastor. Christ gave pastors:

> [F]or the equipping of the saints for the work of ministry, for the edifying of the body of Christ, till we all

come to the unity of the faith and of the knowledge of the Son of God, to a perfect man, to the measure of the stature of the fullness of Christ; that we should no longer be children, tossed to and fro and carried about with every wind of doctrine, by the trickery of men, in the cunning craftiness of deceitful plotting, but speaking the truth in love may grow up in all things into Him who is the head – Christ. (Ephesians 4:12-15)

The pastor's responsibility is that of equipping or preparing every member in the church for ministry (service). The pastor prepares the members to serve Christ, so the church will find strength and purpose in any cultural milieu. With the advent of modern mega-churches, preparing members to fulfill the mission and ministry of the church by pastoral discipleship is almost impossible. A mature church is one where all the members grow up spiritually. As the apostle Paul says, "we all," have a responsibility to grow up spiritually. The depth of a mature church is measured by the unity of faith and the unity of the knowledge of the Son of God.

Faith and knowledge is necessary if one is to mature in the Christian life. Faith means to believe in something that is knowable. Blind faith is logically impossible and unbiblical in doctrine. Since faith requires some knowledge of the object of faith, Christians must have more than just an acquaintance with biblical doctrine. Without faith and knowledge, the church will not mature. Immaturity will disable the church from engaging in the culture in a positive Christian sense.

Particular churches have demonstrated immaturity throughout biblical history. At the root of the immature church, according to the standards and qualifications in the Bible, is the lack of born again, gifted, and educated, pastors/teachers. At the next level, the born again, gifted, and educated pastors/teachers are not doing their jobs. Even if the pastor does his job, the equipped saints may fail to do their jobs. The biblical model is for the equipped pastor to equip the congregation for the work of ministry. Then, the church is ready to influence positively the culture with principles from the Word of God.

The Bible uses four metaphors to describe the immature church. The church acts like a child. For example, a child may play with a poisonous snake, but when the child matures, poisonous snakes are off-limits. Christians come to Christ like a child, but growth follows. Another metaphor describes the immature believer in terms of being tossed back and forth. There is no consistency in doctrine and practice. The immature church is carried about with every wind of doctrine. The immature church is influenced by the trickery of men into doctrinal error. The apostle Paul left the church with this charge.

> Preach the word! Be ready in season and out of season. Convince, rebuke, exhort, with all longsuffering and teaching. For the time will come when they will not endure sound doctrine, but according to their own desires, because they have itching ears, they will heap up for themselves teachers; and they will turn their ears away from the truth, and be turned aside to fables. (2 Timothy 4:2-4)

In the absence of Christian maturity and when everyone does what seems right in his or her own eyes, it is time to cry out to the Lord. The lack of maturity and the consummate individualism provoked God's anger. Those Old Testament saints had no place to turn except to the Lord. The Lord appointed Gideon to save Israel from the impending destruction. I hope you will notice the principle of monarchy at work. When suffering or impending destruction is before us, we, like the Israelites want to hear from a Savior who can save; a Monarch, a King, who has the power to save.

One of the great blessings for Christians is to adopt the principle of monarchy. They need a Monarch or a King who is dependable, trustworthy, merciful, and all-powerful who will speak to His people truthfully. The opposite of the principle of monarchy is individualism. "Every man does what is right in his own eyes." To put it another way, every man is his own god. One stays focused on the creature and the other stays focused on the Creator.

The Lord Jesus Christ suffered and died on the cross for His people so they would be productive and fruitful in the kingdom of God. The Lord equips them with His Word, just as Gideon was equipped with the words from God. I make the distinction that God's Word is much clearer and fuller to successive generations than it was to Gideon. However, the Bible should guide every generation of Christians in every decision of life.

If Christ purchased eternal salvation for your soul with His own blood, then you must reject the evil of individualism and the pride that accompanies it. Rather than every man doing what is right in His own eyes, every man must do what is right in the eyes of God. Pride and self-glory will prevent the church from influencing a godless culture. Too often professing Christians rob God of His glory while the culture watches the hypocrisy. Moralism fades from the eyes of culture because the cultural elites are quick to warn their followers of the covetousness, greed, hatred, and false teaching among professing Christians. What is the solution? The Lord says, "Return to Me…and I will return to you" (Zechariah 1:3).

God's people in every generation since the fall of man, rob God of His glory. Descriptive history from the Word of God reveals worldly methods that tend to replace God's normative instructions. The text in Judges speaks directly about the glory of God and prideful sin of man. When Gideon showed up for battle with 32,000 troops, the Lord said, "you are too many. . .lest Israel claim glory for itself against Me saying 'My own hand has saved me.'" (Judges 7:2).

Do you see the doctrinal and practical implications? "My own hand has saved me" shows a universal sin problem. People want to save themselves. However, the real sin is self-glory resulting from a root sin known as pride. Many men have found their destruction in pride. Pride demands self-glory and God will not permit it.

Gideon was like any other man, he was fearful of the enemy, so he sought the way of the world to succeed. He saw success in numbers. The Bible does not teach there is success in numbers. In fact, the Bible teaches that God usually works through a handful of dedicated men. It was not the 31,700 men who appeared for battle that actually fought the battle. It is not those who act like children in the faith, tossed back and forth by every wind of doctrine or easily tricked by the doctrine of men that will actually advance the kingdom of God. It is maturity and faithfulness that counts.

The enemies of God are the enemies of the children of God. Unless there is a peace treaty, a conflict will ensue. The Bible has a whole chapter on the principles of warfare (Deuteronomy 20). One mandate is applicable to this discussion. "What man is there who is fearful and fainthearted? Let him go and return to his house, lest the heart of his brethren faint like his heart" (Deuteronomy 20:8). In the battle for truth, those who are weak in the Word will be tossed back and forth. God calls His people to believe Him and what He says. The Lord has given His people specific instructions for their engagement in the kingdom of God, which includes the church and the culture. Every man, woman, and child who has been given the gift of faith and eternal life begins his or her walk with Christ as a child in the faith, but he or she will not remain a child. The child of God will grow in maturity in the faith. The child of God will adopt a biblical world and life view. The child of God will not do what appears to be right, unless it is agreeable with the Word of God.

The biblical account of Gideon is quite remarkable. A man of humble means rose to the top to become a great general. On the other hand if a man is born in a royal family and inherits the throne, so what? What credit is it to a man who is born with a silver spoon in his mouth? However, Gideon was not born in this way. He was a farm boy. He "thrashed wheat at the wine press." Even Gideon said, "he was weakest in the tribe of Manassah and the least in his father's household." Those sound like the words of a humble man.

Gideon listened to the Lord, obeyed the Lord and became a great general in Israel. The story of his victory over the Midianites is a story of a great importance to Christians who are engaged with cultural battles. Gideon was a man of diplomatic ability as the evidence indicates in his encounter with the tribe of Ephriam (Judges 8:1-3).

Gideon was a man who knew how to fight, prevail and defeat the enemy. In Judges 8:4-21 there is the account of Gideon and his 300 mighty men, no longer blowing trumpets and waving torches. They are combat troops with a determination to wipe out the enemy. Gideon's 300 men defeated 15,000 Midianites (Judges 8:10). The defeat should not come as a surprise. The Monarch of the Universe gave Gideon his marching orders. "Then the Lord turned to him and said, 'Go in this might of yours, and you shall save Israel and from the hand of the Midianites'" (Judges 6:14). All Gideon had to do is stay focused. However, Gideon's humble beginning and a disposition to obey the Lord dwindled at the end of Gideon's ministry. Gideon seems to shift from reliance on the Lord to his own set of presuppositions.

Many have started their walk with the Lord with humility and a passion to please God, but they did not stay focused. Well begun is not enough. To put it another way, it is not the beginning that counts, it is the end. Take marriage for example. The beginning of marriage usually is full of romance and excitement, but the real test of one's character is how well does he or she finish? It is exciting to prepare, plant, and tend a garden, but does it produce vegetables?

The final years of Gideon's life reveals the true character of Gideon. The people of Israel tempted Gideon with the honor of kingship. Gideon was a great Judge and general for Israel, so the confederacy offered him the crown rights. The offer to be the king of Israel would have been the climax of his glorious career. Gideon was a skillful warrior and a shrewd diplomat. He exercised determination and seemed to be superior in all the abilities needed of a king. For his exercise of leadership, the people of Israel show their gratitude by asking Gideon to rule over them. Gideon refused to serve as the monarch of Israel. Gideon's refusal to accept the position of King of Israel may lead one to believe that Gideon remained faithful to the Lord. "But Gideon said to them, 'I will not rule over you, nor shall my son rule over you; the Lord shall rule over you'" (Judges 8:23).

It sure appears as if Gideon understood the monarchical principle; "the Lord shall rule over you." However, Gideon's statement is descriptive history. A sinner may be able to say the words, but not really mean them. Maybe Gideon pretended to be humble by his words, but in practice, he was not really humble. Was Gideon's humility by mouth or by practice? At the end of his life, he mocked God with his disgraceful sinfulness. One of his sins was his multiple marriages and a concubine (a girlfriend he was sleeping with). The writer of Judges makes mention of Gideon's son, Abimelech, who was born of a concubine. The Hebrew word translated "Abimelech" literally means, "father is king."

Gideon may have refused the offer to be king of Israel as a token of his humble beginning, but there is ample evidence indicating that Gideon acted like a king and even left the mark on his son that indicated Gideon was a king. In the ancient near eastern culture, it was common for pagan kings to have multiple wives, a disgraceful mark on Gideon's final years. The dispute between Abimelech and Gideon's son Jotham over succession rights is another reason to believe that Gideon assumed the place of the king, if not the title. Even the Midianite kings said Gideon resembled a king.

Gideon's wordy refusal sounds good, but his life and character looks bad. The Bible says Gideon made an ephod, which became a snare to Gideon and his household. There is some question as to what the ephod consisted of that Gideon created. It may have been a breastplate like that worn by the high priest or it may have been a freestanding image? In either case, the ephod became an object of worship not only by Gideon and his family, but also by the people. There is every reason to believe that Gideon, at least to some extent, assumed the place of a priest. He may have been a great general, but he was a bad priest. King Saul made the same fatal error. It takes more than an ephod or an animal sacrifice to make a priest. Gideon did not stay focused on serving God. The culture consumed Gideon with customs, behavior, and false worship.

There are professing Christian men and women who are brave and bold like Gideon. They are angry against some of the moral wrongs in their culture. They take up armor against the enemy, but they make the same fatal mistake that Gideon made. They set out against the evil, but they use their own plans and devices.

God has given his Word to guide and direct His people. The principles in His Word are temporally and eternally important. Staying focused is a principle found in the Word of God. For instance, the Psalmist explains the principle. "Unto You I lift up my eyes, O You who dwell in the heavens. Behold, as the eyes of servants look to the hand of their masters, as the eyes of a maid to the hand of her mistress, so our eyes look to the LORD our God, until He has mercy on us" (Psalm 123:1-2).

Christians in the modern culture, the postmodern culture, or any cultural milieu yet to be announced may not have ephods to worship nor high priests to compete with However, they have their own idols and their own desires. One of the most popular Psalms is Psalm twenty-three. Many Christians can quote it or at least a portion of it. The first verse has a principle that is largely ignored by the church, "The Lord is my Shepherd; I shall not want." The principle that stands out is the sufficiency of God, thus there is no need for idols or any kind of false worship.

Christians individually and churches collectively are busy building ephods to worship while they say with their mouth, "The Lord is my Shepherd; I shall not want." The professing Evangelical church has a history of fabricating all sorts of schemes that are nothing more than ephods. During the 19th century, Charles Finney introduced the "anxious bench" as the place that sinners would venture to for the conversion experience. By the beginning of the 21st century, it is called an "alter call." This unbiblical "ephod" fabricated by preachers is not necessary for salvation. Yet, it has virtually become an object of worship at worst or an object of faith at best. The church is quick to start one unbiblical program after the other. The list is endless and they are nothing but ephods.

Many professing Christians started on a solid course; so did Gideon. Many evangelical denominations and seminaries started with the right purpose; so did Gideon. Unfortunately many end in disaster because they do not stay focused on God's plan and God's will.

8. Staying Focused

Will you be able to say like the apostle Paul:

I have fought the good fight,
I have finished the race,
I have kept the faith. (2 Tim. 4:7)

9.   Stealthy Deception

Then Abimelech the son of Jerubbaal went to Shechem, to his mother's brothers, and spoke with them and with all the family of the house of his mother's father, saying, "Please speak in the hearing of all the men of Shechem: 'Which is better for you, that all seventy of the sons of Jerubbaal reign over you, or that one reign over you?' Remember that I am your own flesh and bone." And his mother's brothers spoke all these words concerning him in the hearing of all the men of Shechem; and their heart was inclined to follow Abimelech, for they said, "He is our brother." So they gave him seventy shekels of silver from the temple of Baal-Berith, with which Abimelech hired worthless and reckless men; and they followed him. Then he went to his father's house at Ophrah and killed his brothers, the seventy sons of Jerubbaal, on one stone. But Jotham the youngest son of Jerubbaal was left, because he hid himself. And all the men of Shechem gathered together, all of Beth Millo, and they went and made Abimelech king beside the terebinth tree at the pillar that was in Shechem.

Judges 9:1-6

The distance between truth and falsehood is not very far, if reality is not important. Sometimes God's truth is painful, because it brings reality, eternal reality, to the attention of Christians. Unbelievers do not like the idea that sin is a reality. They may retaliate if threatened by the consequences of sin. Dr. John Gerstner told the story of Jonathan Edwards preaching on hell, sin, judgment and eternal punishment to the congregation. Gerstner explained that the people hated God, but since they could not put their hands on God, they tried to get rid of Jonathan Edwards. However, it is gratifying to know that godly believing people find comfort in the same words that the unbeliever hears and finds discomfort.

The story of Abimelech in the book of Judges may bring pain or comfort, but it will not leave you indifferent. Abimelech was Gideon's son by a concubine who lived in Shechem. Gideon was one of the better judges in the Israelite confederacy, but still a man of questionable scruples.

It was Gideon who said to the children of Israel, "I will not rule over you, nor shall my son rule over you; the Lord shall rule over you." However, it appears that Gideon lived like a king and his prophecy was not exactly true. God used Gideon to overthrow the Midianites and the Bible asserts, "The country was quiet for forty years in the days of Gideon. Then Gideon died."

The historical pattern in Israel during the period of the Judges was that after a judge died, "the children would again do evil in the sight of the Lord." The Bible explains, "as soon as Gideon was dead, that the children of Israel again played the harlot with the Baals and made Baal-Berith their god. Thus the children of Israel did not remember the Lord their God, who had saved them" (Judges 8:33). Then the people of Israel cried out to the Lord and the Lord would raise up a deliverer to save them.

In the early chapters of Judges the Lord raised up a deliverer or to put it another way, the Lord raised up a savior for the repentant Old Testament church. However, after the death of Gideon, the children of Israel did not cry out and the Lord did not send a deliverer. The events that followed revealed the stealthy deception of Gideon's son, Abimelech. The application of this portion of God's Word is simple and repeated throughout history. Replace the name Abimelech with _____. Simply fill in the blank with a name that thinks and acts like Abimelech.

The ambitious son of Gideon wanted the power, honor, and glory of his father. The love of power and supremacy consumed Abimelech. He was an ambitious man, but it was a wicked and evil ambition. His wickedness is manifestly clear. He thought he was more important than other people; especially more important than the other sons of Gideon. Abimelech did not follow the monarchical principle; he did not seek counsel from God's Word to determine his course of action.

Abimelech was the kind of man that knew the art of stealthiness. His cunning insinuations, his deceitful promise, and his flattering speech would hoodwink a whole city into believing that he was a savior. Abimelech's campaign speech to the people of Shechem reveals the art of a sophist. Abimelech said, "Which is better for you, that all seventy of the sons of Jerubbaal reign over you, or that one reign over you? Remember I am your own flesh and bone" (Judges 9:2). Abimelech's stealth was rooted in a worldview known as sophism. The dictionary describes stealth as, "Not disclosing one's true ideology, affiliations, or positions." For example, a liberal theologian may say, "I believe in the resurrection of Jesus Christ." It is a statement that sounds strictly orthodox. However, if the liberal theologian were pressed with the question, "Do you believe in the bodily resurrection of Jesus Christ?" the answer would be, "No!"

In early Greek philosophy, sophism was a worldview that employed specious arguments to deceive someone. Sophism was the basis for deception; stealth was the practice of sophism. Paul the apostle was trained to defend the truth against stealthy deception. The pursuit of truth was considered a virtue in Paul's day. However, at the beginning of the 21st century, poll after poll indicates that if there is any truth, it does not matter. Perhaps the stealthy deception of sophism is the reason why so many Christian leaders convincingly get away with not telling the truth. Parents admonish their children to tell the truth, but adults laugh at little white lies. The enemy of truth in any generation is the evil art of sophistry. The first Christian scholar was probably Clement of Alexandria. Although little is known of his life, he was one of the early defenders of the Christian religion. In one his writings he said explained the principle of sophism.

> The art of sophistry, which the Greeks cultivated, is a fantastic power, which makes false opinions like true by means of words. For it produces rhetoric in order to persuasion, and disputation for wrangling. These arts, therefore, if not conjoined with philosophy, will be injurious to every one. For Plato openly called sophistry "an evil art." And Aristotle, following him, demonstrates it to be a dishonest art, which abstracts in a specious manner the whole business of wisdom, and professes a wisdom which it has not studied. (*Stromata*, Clement of Alexandria, book 1, chapter 8)

Sophistry is a subtle false argument. To sophisticate means to mislead by deception and false arguments. To be sophisticated is actually bad, although a revised contemporary meaning is that a sophisticated person is worldly wise, mature, classy, in the know, and on top of all situations. If the root word "sophism" is an enemy to truth, how can its derivative word "sophisticated" be good for truth? For instance, worldly wise does not necessarily express truth.

The history of Christianity reveals the presence of sophism in every generation. In the 16th century, John Calvin said:

> The argument against Christianity unfolds itself and discloses the tangled web of their sophistries, men of discernment see at once that what they have apprehended is nothing at all. I see that the world everywhere trifles with God, and that the ungodly delude themselves with Sophistries. (*Calvin's Commentary on Nahum*)

The 19th century Presbyterian theologian, James H. Thornwell said, "The sophist of speculation is the hypocrite." Sophism and stealthy deception always has and always will be an enemy to any church for every generation and all cultures.

In the text of Acts 24 and 25, Paul makes his defense before Felix the governor of Judea. The Jews from Jerusalem came to charge Paul with the hope that Felix would turn Paul over to them or better yet that Felix would have Paul put to death. The Jewish leaders from Jerusalem brought a spokesman with them. His name was Tertullus. Whether he was a Jew or Roman Lawyer is speculative. He appears to have been knowledgeable with Roman law and has a Roman name. Felix the governor called on Tertullus to state his case.

In the typical style of that day, Tertullus should acknowledge the governor's office and authority. Notice how Tertullus addressed the governor. Tertullus accredited Felix with bringing peace and prosperity to Judea. That was a lie, a big lie. Felix brought trouble, dissension, suspension, and terror to that part of the Middle East. Then Tertullus said Felix was a man of foresight. That was a lie. Family connections and intrigue got him the position. His corruption caused so much trouble that Nero finally recalled Felix. Tertullus skillfully lied, as any sophist does, to gain favor with the governor.

Tertullus eventually said there were three charges against Paul. First, Paul was charged with being a trouble-maker. In the New King James Version, the phrase "creator of dissension" derives from a Greek word that is related to the English word "plague". The sophisticated and stealthy charge is that Paul's doctrine was like an infectious disease. It would spread throughout the empire. It was alleged that Paul's doctrine was a real danger for the Roman Empire. Second, Paul was charged with being a ringleader of the sect of the Nazarenes. A ringleader is always considered a threat by the state. Third, Tertullus said Paul tried to desecrate the Temple. Of the three charges, this is the only one of significance. Rome had given the Jews permission to impose the death penalty to anyone who defiled the temple. All three charges were merely accusations. However, they were very effectively presented by way of sophistry and deceptive stealth.

Tertullus stated these points as if they were true and ultimately deserved condemnation. Tertullus concluded his arguments with an agreement from the Jews present. He told Felix, "by examining him yourself you may ascertain all these things of which we accuse him." Tertullus assumed that his deception and cunning was believable. Felix should believe the charges because Tertullus made them, the Jews present for the trial agreed and the democracy, that is the mob at Jerusalem, had voted against Paul.

There was no place for truth, but the sophist forgot a fundamental axiom. Truth is always true even if nobody believes it. Falsehood is false even if everybody believes it. Os Guinness has rightly said, "Without truth we are all vulnerable to manipulation."

Paul's defense before Felix was radically and truthfully different from the deceptive rhetoric of Tertullus. Paul clearly stated that he was not a troublemaker. He was only in Jerusalem for six days. He did not even preach while he was there. Paul disputed no one while he was there. He did not even gather a crowd of people except the democracy without a conscience.

Paul admitted he was a follower of the way, but certainly not a ringleader. Anyhow, Roman law allowed Paul to practice his religion just as it allowed the Jews to practice their religion. Paul's final defense was, "I did not desecrate the temple." In fact, Paul was submitting to the Jewish law and was ceremonially clean. There was no sophistry in Paul's defense. There was no stealthy deception. There was no wrangling with words. Truth was Paul's only defense. A nation that gives in to the deception of sophistry by stealth, will lose the freedom to tell the truth. Abimelech's argument was a sophisticated stealthy argument. His argument was simple:

> One ruler is better than seventy rulers scattered over the territory;
>
> I am a hometown boy;
>
> Therefore, you can believe me even if my argument is wrong.

Satan tried deceiving the Lord Jesus Christ in the same way. Satan tried to convince Jesus, with very crafty language, to disregard reality. To put it another way, do not pay attention to that which is true. Abimelech played on the pity of people in Shechem to divert their attention away from God's covenant promises. He tried to convince and actually does deceive them for a while that blood is thicker than truth. A jealous, prideful, ambitious man, controlled by the power of Satan, dupes the people of Shechem into believing that he should be the king.

Abimelech used bloodshed and savagery to climb the ladder of success. There are many examples of Abimelech today. The methods are less scandalous in some ways, but still reflect the cursed ambition of this wicked world. Abimelech or whatever name you might substitute, will visit every church and culture and every generation.

Abimelech was a man of treachery. He convinced the men of Shechem to give him money so he could hire thugs to kill all the other children of Gideon. He simply wanted to get rid of anyone who threatened his ambitious spirit. He almost accomplished what he set out to do. He got rid of all the opposition except one, the youngest son of Gideon. Jotham, the youngest son of Gideon, escaped the murdering hand of Abimelech.   Since there was no opposition, the men of Shechem crowned Abimelech king.

However, the truth was about to emerge.   The coronation of Abimelech, with all the festive activities, the pomp and the ostentatious pageantry were met with the appearance of young Jotham.   Standing above them on Mt. Gerizim Jotham lifted his voice to the crowd of heathens below. The courageous young man said, "Listen to me, you men of Shechem, That God may listen to you."

He told them a parable of the trees that went to crown a tree over all the trees. The trees of the forest, presumably the cedar tree, the oak tree, the beech tree, the palm tree, the fir tree and maybe a pine tree. All these trees went to the olive tree and asked the olive tree to be their king. The olive tree refused the leadership position. The olive tree was a very valuable tree. The olive tree was aware of its special place, with its special gifts, and refused to leave that which honored God and men. Then all the trees went to the fig tree and said, "be our king." However, the fig tree refused saying, "should I cease my sweetness and my good fruit?" The fig tree was one of the most important trees in Palestine and if the tree could speak for itself in this parable it would surely say, "I don't want to become fruitless." In an attempt to get a leader, all the trees said to the vine: You be our king. The grapevine said: "Should I cease my new wine, which cheers both God and men, just to say I'm the king?" Finally, the trees said to the bramble, "You come and rule over us." Can you imagine that? All the lofty trees of the forest asked the disrespectable bramble to rule over the forest. The bramble is a low bushy tree with thorns and its wood is easily set a fire so that it causes the forest to burn up.

~~The trees finally found a king. The unqualified~~ bramble accepted the crown without any deliberation. Even though the bramble has no fatness like the olive tree or any sweetness like the fig tree or any rich clusters like the vine, the trees were duped into crowning the bramble bush as their king. The bramble bush has no shadow and offers nothing but painful thorns and burning fire, yet the trees wanted him as king. The other trees are to be commended for not giving up a useful and productive calling. However, the trees acted stupidly by calling the incompetent and potentially dangerous bramble bush to be their king.

> Jotham wanted the people to know that their choice for a king was a mistake because Abimelech was a worthless disreputable character. As one theologian has said, "brambles make good fuel, but poor kings" (*Judges: Such a Great Salvation*, Dale Ralph Davis, p. 123)

People seem to prefer bramble leadership rather than competent and worthy leadership. One who lived to write about the Nazi Party celebration in 1934 describes the charm of Hitler's words.

> The words he uttered, the thoughts he expressed, often seemed to be ridiculous, but that week in Nuremberg I began to comprehend that it did not matter so much what he said, but how he said it. Hitler's communication with his audiences was uncanny. He established a rapport almost immediately and deepened and intensified it as he went on speaking, holding them completely in his spell. In such a state, it seemed to me, they easily believed anything he said, even the most foolish nonsense. Over the years as I listened to scores of Hitler's major speeches, I would pause in my own mind to exclaim, "What utter rubbish! What brazen lies!" Then I would look around at the audience. His

German listeners were lapping up every word as the utter truth (*Judges: Such a Great Salvation*, Ralph Dale Davis, p. 124).

For thousands of years, people in western civilization have used words to persuade, gain power, and to deceive. The church is just as guilty as the culture. The opposite of deceit is truth.

Jotham finished his parable and concluded his remarks with a prophecy. It is a prophecy with this contingency: "if you have acted in truth and sincerity." If the people of Shechem acted in truth and sincerity in respect to Gideon and his family, then they may look forward to a good government under Abimelech. Unfortunately, they had not acted in truth and sincerity. In fact, the curse of ambition fell upon those wicked Shechemites. The period during the time of the Judges was one of chaos, confusion, anarchy, and tyranny. However, Israel was not always in a state of chaos, because sometimes God gave them peace in the land. There was a mixture of anarchy and tyranny, however it was locally and occasionally. Judges chapter nine is a historical account of the period during which Abimelech, a son of Gideon, was a tyrant.

Jotham warned the people to remember the fundamental rule necessary for intelligent discussion and trustworthiness among equals. The fundamental rule is truth and truth must have substantial authority. Jotham, unlike his wicked brother Abimelech, was truthful with the people of Shechem.

Truth and sincerity were important to Jotham. Likewise, truth and sincerity are especially important for God's people to have any kind of intellectual discourse. The word sincerity was used in the early part of the 17th century when the King James Version was given to the English-speaking world. At that time, the word sincerity may have been appropriate. However, now it is not. Sincerity essentially refers to honesty. For example, the majority of professing conservative, evangelicals teach that God sincerely desires all men to be saved. You must pause and ask the question, "What does it mean for God to sincerely want something?" If God is sincere or honest, then God cannot possibly with absolute honesty desire something that would violate His nature and character. If God insincerely desires something that does violate his nature and character, then God would be a hypocrite. It is blasphemous to think or even intimate that God is a hypocrite. Therefore, God cannot sincerely or honestly want for something that He is perfectly capable of bringing to pass.

Sadly, in the 21st century postmodern world, the word sincerity is most often associated with the affections. For instance, I've heard people say things like, "I'd sincerely love to see welfare and many other give-away statist programs come to an end." If the sophism and stealthy deception is removed, few are the people who sincerely or "in reality" want to bring those federally funded programs to an end. The direct recipients want to receive the federal funds and the indirect recipients, the businesses receiving the benefit of sales, want the direct recipients to trade with them. The truth is that only a few sincerely want anything other than personal happiness and pleasure.

Truth and honesty are necessary for a lasting and prosperous relationship, either personally or in a society or in the church and especially in the church. Abimelech and the people of Shechem turned against each other. "God sent a spirit of ill will between Abimelech and the men of Shechem; and the men of Shechem dealt treacherously with Abimelech" (Judges 9:23).

When treachery is involved in a relationship, there you will find deceit and unfaithfulness. Treachery means that truth has been abandoned in favor of expediency or pragmatism, or in the case of Abimelech, because the curse of self-ambition became the controlling factor. Abimelech was a liar to start with even though his lies were convincing too many of the people. However, Abimelech's influence was local and occasional. The real danger for any nation is when the Abimelech world and life view becomes national and permanent.

A liar will eventually be caught in his or her lie. Abimelech's deceitfulness caught up with him in three short years. Whether it is three years or three hundred years, you may be assured that liars and deceivers will get their pay from the hand of a just God.

Abimelech was in control for a while and had loyal followers. However, you can be assured that anytime a person deals treacherously, there is another deceiver who is ready to deal treacherously against the other person. In Shechem there was a man named Gaal who, like Abimelech was an opportunist. Suffice it to say, Gaal was an ambitious man. For the sake of clarity, let me recapitulate the story of Abimelech, Gaal, and the people of Shechem.

The same people who crowned Abimelech, wanted to dethrone him and make Gaal their leader. Abimelech resented the move, came to Shechem, destroyed the citizens and sowed the city with salt. Sowing with salt was symbolic of a barren wasteland. Abimelech showed those Shechemites who was boss. During his raid at Shechem, the people ran into a tower for safety. Abimelech burned the people alive, about one thousand of them according to the Bible (Judges 9:49).

Abimelech was a pragmatist. He tried to burn the people at Thebez because it worked at Shechem, but a woman dropped a big rock on Abimelech's head. The rock did not quite kill Abimelech, so he asked his armor bearer to finish him off, so history would not reveal that a woman killed the low down scoundrel. The life of Abimelech reminds us of how much a price must be paid when treachery, sophism, and stealthy deception is a way of life. Wickedness has a price tag that exceeds the budget of any living human being.

The people of Shechem were punished because of their wickedness. Abimelech was punished because of his wickedness. The irony is that God used both parties to destroy each other. Evil destroyed evil. The Lord will see to it that His righteousness will be vindicated.

There is ample evidence that the visible church and the culture around the church, has a large supply of Abimelech's, Gaal's, Zebul's, and ungodly men like those of Shechem. Abimelech killed one thousand people in the temple and some of those people probably had no interest in the squabble between Abimelech and Gaal. The lesson to learn is that one evil man or woman in the church or the culture may bring pain and suffering to a much larger number.

With the remaining spirit of modernity and postmodernity following closely on its heels, the church should beware of all the wickedness of the present culture. I believe, and unless convinced otherwise, I will continue to teach and write with fervent passion against egalitarianism, anti-intellectualism, multiculturalism, relativism, and a whole host of other evils that prevail and are destroying the church and the culture.

10. Frivolous Words

Then the Spirit of the LORD came upon Jephthah, and he passed through Gilead and Manasseh, and passed through Mizpah of Gilead; and from Mizpah of Gilead he advanced toward the people of Ammon. And Jephthah made a vow to the LORD, and said, "If You will indeed deliver the people of Ammon into my hands, then it will be that whatever comes out of the doors of my house to meet me, when I return in peace from the people of Ammon, shall surely be the LORD's, and I will offer it up as a burnt offering." So Jephthah advanced toward the people of Ammon to fight against them, and the LORD delivered them into his hands. And he defeated them from Aroer as far as Minnith—twenty cities—and to Abel Keramim, with a very great slaughter. Thus the people of Ammon were subdued before the children of Israel. When Jephthah came to his house at Mizpah, there was his daughter, coming out to meet him with timbrels and dancing; and she was his only child. Besides her he had neither son nor daughter. And it came to pass, when he saw her, that he tore his clothes, and said, "Alas, my daughter! You have brought me very low! You are among those who trouble me! For I have given my word to the LORD, and I cannot go back on it."

Judges 11:29-35

Tola and Jair were Judges after Abimelech. Neither of them seemed to perform any special deeds. They simply judged Israel during a relatively peaceful time in Israel. The old song, "Be Happy, Don't Worry" describes the Old Testament church and the culture at that time. It appears that the Israelites were happy during the time of Tola and Jair, so happy they forgot about the true and living God who would soon enough judge them.

The church and culture at the beginning of the 21st century is in a similar situation. Most of society lives and dies with state money and the state is considered god. Many

Citizens do whatever the state says for fear of losing their entitlement program. "Hey, everybody's happy and everything's good" are the sentiments of a majority of the people in the United States.

The book of Judges is a harbinger to modern history. Moral and spiritual degradation of each succeeding generation is predictable as per our study of the Book of Judges. Every generation in modern history becomes worse than the former generation. The Enlightenment was supposed to have saved the western world by using the scientific method, the absconding of the metaphysical by Immanuel Kant, the rising force of modernity and the most recent appearance of post modernity. These and many other emerging humanistic ideas cause me to wonder what will happen to all the local particular churches around the world as each period of time establishes new deceptions for the church?

The increase of sin and wickedness tends to bring God's wrath to earth in the form of chaos, calamity and misery. Particular visible churches have not escaped God's righteous right hand.

Consumerism is a worldview that captured the mind of western civilization during the 20th century. Satan uses consumerism to give people, especially professing Christians, a sense of false security. He tricks them into thinking that material prosperity is the source of all happiness. It is merely a diversion to keep people from facing reality. Satan's diversions lead people deeper into idolatry, so that idolatry becomes the chief sin of the masses. The object of worship is the prerogative of every individual and often blends all too comfortably with the secular cultural milieu.

Idolatry always begins in small doses. While Tola and Jair judged Israel, there appeared to be peace and prosperity, but look at what happened at the end of 45 years. Israel not only worshipped Baal and Asherah, they worshipped every god in the land. "Then the children of Israel again did evil in the sight of the LORD, and served the Baals and the Ashtoreths, the gods of Syria, the gods of Sidon, the gods of Moab, the gods of the people of Ammon, and the gods of the Philistines; and they forsook the LORD and did not serve Him" (Judges 10:6). The Moabites worshipped Chemosh (1 Kings 11:3), the Ammonites worshipped Milcom (1 Kings 11:5), and the Philistines worshipped Dagon (Judges 16:23). The Israelites worshipped (consumed) all of them. People tend to worship according to their inclinations. They worship what they desire.

The Old Testament church desired to worship Baal, Chemosh, Milcom, and Dagon along with their worship to the true and living God. God punished the people of Israel because of idolatry. "He sold them into the hands of the Philistines and into the hands of the people of Ammon" (Judges 10:7). God's people wanted to worship all the gods that the culture worshipped and worship the one only living and true God. They wanted the best of both worlds.

God will not permit dichotomous allegiance. In fact, God will punish a divided allegiance. Jesus addressed this principle without mincing words. "No one can serve two masters; for either he will hate the one and love the other, or else he will be loyal to the one and despise the other. You cannot serve God and mammon" (Matthew 6:24). God commands His church to "put away the foreign gods." False doctrine is a foreign god, perhaps the most dangerous foreign god as it erodes the base. Christians must put it out of the church, so the culture will take notice. Ungodly tradition is a foreign god. The tradition I have in mind is tradition that has no merit from the Word of God. Jesus said to the Jews, "You nicely set aside the commandment of God in order to keep your tradition" (Mark. 7:8). Over the past thirty years, I have witnessed church disputes over tradition (we've always done it this way) that always damages the witness of the church.

The culture takes notice of the conflicts and uses them to disgrace the church. Christians must put tradition out of the church, so the culture will believe God's people are a principled and united people. The church must speak the truth found in the Word of God so that the culture may understand the meaning of principles that affect their welfare. The church must speak, as if it is God speaking to the culture.

Speech is the result of the rational soul expressing intelligent communication. Speech is formulated from the use of words. The logic of language is one of the most neglected disciplines in the western culture. "Words are trifles, to most men. They have heard them too often. It is all fake, advertising, propaganda, lying. Indeed it is. But why is there so much abuse of language" (*Speech and Reality*, by Eugen Rosenstock-Huessy, p. 46). Jesus answered that question when he spoke the truth to the Pharisees.

> For out of the abundance of the heart the mouth speaks. A good man out of the good treasure of his heart brings forth good things, and an evil man out of the evil treasure brings forth evil things. But I say to you that for every idle word men may speak, they will give account of it in the day of judgment. For by your words you will be justified, and by your words you will be condemned. (Matthew 12:34-37)

The words we speak have eternal consequences. Rosenstock-Hussey applies this to culture. "Man must speak if he wishes to have a society; but very often he cannot speak and then his society breaks down" (*The Origin of Speech*, by Eugen Rosenstock-Huessy, p. 32).

The life of Jephthah in the Book of Judges will help Christians understand the value of words that lead to articulate speech or the misuse of words that lead to inarticulate speech. Jephthah was born into a strained relationship, because his father committed adultery. Jephthah was chased away from his city and his family inheritance because of his father's adulterous relationship. Jephthah developed a relationship in his new environment, but with a bunch of thugs and thieves. All the while, the Israelites were having relationship problems with the surrounding nations, especially Ammon. They had an army, but they did not have a leader. The people of Gilead wanted someone to command them, rather than every man doing what was right in his own eyes.

The city of Gilead sought the leadership of a man that had been chased out of their fair city. The elders of Gilead allowed the brothers of Jephthah to banish him, but when they needed his help, they could not get to him fast enough. The people had no use for Jephthah during the good times, but when hard times came, Jephthah was recalled. Speech entered in the conflict of two cultures. Jephthah said, "Did you not hate me, and expel me from my father's house? Why have you come to me now when you are in distress?" (Judges 11:7).

Jephthah did forgive the people and made a contract with them to be their commander and judge. In return, the elders of Gilead made a biblical oath to ratify the covenant. The strangest aspect of this relationship between Jephthah and the elders of Gilead is that they both chose their words in a fashion that reflects the utmost care. So far, in the book of Judges, there has been no mention of diplomacy. Jephthah used words to circumvent a war against the Ammonites. Jephthah's logic and rhetorical skills should not go unnoticed. He argued from history that the land did not belong to the Ammonites. He argued from theology that God had given the Israelites possession of the land by covenant. He argued from precedent that the Moabite king at the time of Israel's settlement in the land did not go to war. Finally, he argued from silence saying the Israelites had been there 300 years and the

Ammonites had not tried to recover the land. Jephthah used sound words to develop sound arguments. Speech was the instrument used in an attempt to avert war with the wicked Ammonites. "However, the king of the people of Ammon did not heed the words which Jephthah sent him" (Judges 11:28). Speech is the forefront of peace or war. I can understand why unbelievers ignore words, but I cannot understand why Christians ignore words. It is words that establish and nourish your relationships both in the secular and in the sacred.

Jephthah is an example of a man who was born into a world of insanity, instability, and iniquity. Jephthah used words to avert war. His speech included words with sound logic and appropriate rules of rhetoric. The Ammonites ignored the arguments, so war was inevitable.

Then Jephthah made a ridiculous vow. Jephthah made a vow to the LORD, and said, "If You will indeed deliver the people of Ammon into my hands, then it will be that whatever comes out of the doors of my house to meet me, when I return in peace from the people of Ammon, shall surely be the LORD's, and I will offer it up as a burnt offering" (Judges 11:30-31).

Jephthah did not need to make a vow relative to his military endeavor against Ammon. God had already equipped Jephthah to fight and win the battle against the Ammonites. A vow was not necessary on this occasion, and the vow Jephthah made was a sinful vow. Theologians have penned gallons of ink writing about Jephthah's vow. Most of the ink was wasted because the biblical text speaks plain and forthright. The English text, "whatever comes out of the doors of my house," could be translated, "whoever comes out, "which is, to my mind, the more accurate translation. Literally, the Hebrew text could be translated, "the one coming out, he comes out from the doors of my house." Common sense tells you that Jephthah would not expect a dog, a goat, or a bull to come out of his house to meet him. There is no reason to believe that Jephthah had a common animal in mind. It would be natural to sacrifice not just one animal upon a victorious win, but to sacrifice many animals. If Jephthah had a human being in mind, he thought that the household servants, of whom he probably had many, would greet him upon his return. A man like Jephthah who lived in an unstable, ungodly, and vicious culture might not have any scruples about an occasional human sacrifice. He knew the "how" to speak with skill, but from an evil heart comes evil words. Human sacrifice was a common practice among the Moabites and there is sufficient evidence to believe that the Ammonites and Moabites were closely connected in religious cult worship. Therefore, I expect Jephthah was influenced to sacrifice a human being because the Ammonites practiced the same horrible sin.

Jephthah was a winner with his words when he used words logically, coherently, and rhetorically. He was compelling and circumvented a war against the Ammonites. However, he was a loser with his words when he stupidly used words to make an unnecessary and unlawful vow. It was bad enough that he made the vow, but to carry out an unlawful vow even compounds his sin. Jephthah sacrificed his daughter, because he did not think ahead as a leader should. He was a loser because either he did not know the Word of God or he did not believe the Word of God. In either case, he was a pitiful loser, because his words ended his family line with the death of his daughter.

The Word of God reveals the fundamental principle that speech is the index of the mind. If the Holy Spirit has regenerated your heart's mind so that you are able to profess faith in Jesus Christ, then your words should match your profession. Jesus said, "from within, out of the heart of men, proceed evil thoughts, adulteries, fornications, murders, thefts, covetousness, wickedness, deceit, lewdness, an evil eye, blasphemy, pride, foolishness" (Mark 7:21-22). Speech reveals the condition of the heart.

Jephthah was not the only person to misuse words, when he probably knew better. I remind you of the Apostle Peter standing outside in the courtyard waiting to the see the outcome of the trial of the Lord Jesus Christ. It was just a few hours before that Peter had told the Lord, "Even if I have to die with You, I will not deny You." A young slave girl accused Peter saying, You also were with Jesus of Galilee and Peter denied it saying; "I do not know the man" (Matthew 26:69-75). Three times Peter used these horrendous words, but we should be quick to add that Peter later repented of his sin. The saints of God are not perfect in this life and neither are their words.

When Israel was about to fall into the hands of the great King Nebuchadnezzar, the Lord spoke to the people of Israel through the prophet Jeremiah about words and truth. (See Jeremiah chapters seven and eight for the full text). The main points are:

1. Truth has perished and has been cut off from their mouth.

2. The prophets hold fast to deceit.

3. The false pen of the scribe certainly works falsehood.

4. Everyone deals falsely.

Those words spoken to the Old Testament church are relevant to the New Testament church. A corrupt evil mind has no interest in truth. If there is no interest in truth, then words are meaningless. Only when words convey truth do they have any meaning at all.

Words are often wasted. Many a war has been fought over a few words. For instance, during the period of the Judges, Ephraim was an arrogant tribe. They wanted to be the center of attention. They wanted other people to notice them. They thought they were so important. The Ephraimites came to Jephthah after he had already defeated the Ammonites and complained because they were not invited to the battlefield. They used words to file their complaint, but according to Jephthah, the Ephraimites lied. Jephthah said he called for help from the Ephraimites, but they did not come and fight.

I am not sure why the Ephraimites raised such a fuss, because Jephthah's influence did not appear to extend beyond Gilead. It could have been the Ephraimites were afraid that Jephthah's rule might extend to the east and encompass the Ephraimites. Anyhow, Ephraim wasted words that resulted in a civil war. Jephthah and the people of Gilead defeated the Ephraimites and captured the strategic crossing places of the Jordan.

Just think about the implications. Two tribes were ensnarled in a bloody battle because of a few wasted words. The result was Israelites killing Israelites. It all started because of insulting and slanderous words. The self-righteous arrogant and flippant big mouth of Ephraim was the straw that broke the camel's back. Taunting the Gileadites as fugitives or runaways caused a lot of blood to spill. One word became the source of death or life. The Bible is self-explanatory.

Now Jephthah gathered together all the men of Gilead and fought against Ephraim. And the men of Gilead defeated Ephraim, because they said, "You Gileadites are fugitives of Ephraim among the Ephraimites and among the Manassites." The Gileadites seized the fords of the Jordan before the Ephraimites arrived.

And when any Ephraimite who escaped said, "Let me cross over," the men of Gilead would say to him, "Are you an Ephraimite?" If he said, "No," then they would say to him, "Then say, '*Shibboleth*'!" And he would say, "*Sibboleth*," for he could not pronounce it right. Then they would take him and kill him at the fords of the Jordan. There fell at that time forty-two thousand Ephraimites. (Judges 12:4-6)

A brief recapitulation of this event may help understand how words are very important. Jephthah stationed guards at the crossing places of the Jordan River and devised a word game that proved very successful for the Gileadites. When an Ephraimite approached a crossing at the Jordan River, a simple password was required for the Ephraimite to pass successfully into the territory of Ephraim. If anyone wanted to the cross the Jordan and denied that he was an Ephraimite, he was given a simple test. He was asked to say the Hebrew word *shibboleth*. The Ephraimite could not say *shibboleth*; he could only say *sibboleth*.

The poor Ephraimites wanted to escape, but upon reaching a crossing place, the Gileadite soldier would say, "Are you an Ephraimite?" No doubt, many said "Oh no, I'm with the tribe of Ruben. Then please say *shibboleth*." But, because of their dialect, the Ephraimite could only say *sibboleth*. The pronouncing of one letter in one word would decide whether or not that person would live or die. One word became the test for life or death.

Phenomenal as this may seem, there is something about that scenario that is beyond the sensible world. Think about this tragedy. A poor Ephraimite, probably deceived by some slick-talking prophet from his tribe, wants to cross the Jordan so he can go back home. In the process, it seems as if he is being betrayed by his own words or should I say, word. When one announces his own death with a word that is supposed to bring life, it makes me wonder. Forty two thousand Old Testament church members slaughtered, many of whom filled the Jordan with their blood, because of one word; One word mind you!!!!

The church has suffered because of the misuse of words. During medieval Christianity, William of Ockham, taught the church that words are mental realities and are universal only to the extent that a word stands for many things. You need not understand the technical and philosophical overtones, just that the church has always wrangled over words. Now in the 20th century, the postmodern literary deconstructionism teaches that any text must be liberated or deconstructed, that is, freed from the authors prejudiced cultural and social baggage.

What does all this tell us? Whether one lived in the 14th century B. C. with Jephthah or the 12th century A.D. with Ockham or the 21st century postmodern deconstructionism, words will either be useful and bring life or be destructive and bring death. We should listen carefully to the words from God. Think of how many thousands of words we use in one day. Now think about what one word - *shibboleth* - can do. A word can murder innocent life or it can preserve life.

11. Accommodation and Compromise

So the woman came and told her husband, saying, "A Man of God came to me, and His countenance was like the countenance of the Angel of God, very awesome; but I did not ask Him where He was from, and He did not tell me His name. And He said to me, "Behold, you shall conceive and bear a son. Now drink no wine or similar drink, nor eat anything unclean, for the child shall be a Nazirite to God from the womb to the day of his death."

Judges 13:6-7

There is a synonym for the "dangers of accommodation." It is the "dangers of compromise." Especially dangerous is reducing God's standard to accommodate the culture. The trend throughout the 20th and now into the 21st century has been to accommodate God's standards to the point of harmony with lower spiritual, moral and ethical standards. To accommodate the culture will lead to more accommodation. I am sure you have heard the old saying, "Things go from bad to worse." This is the sinful nature of man.

Christians enjoy mountain top experiences, but they descend from the mountain top to the valley below. There are times when societies, cultures, and nations demonstrate respect for authority, honor, and dignity. There are other times when those qualities are like precious gems, very hard to find. An Israelite during the period of the Judges may have said, "things are going from bad to worse," as many Christians say today!

The leaders of Israel judged Israel because even though Israel was a theocracy (ruled by God), they were still a secular confederacy. They did not have one king to rule over them. The author of Judges reminds the church that individualism is ever present. "In those days there was no king in Israel; everyone did what was right in his own eyes" (Judges

17:6). God's people were rebellious and God punished them by giving them what they wanted. Their desire was to worship the idols and false gods of the other nations. Since they desired false worship, God allowed them to be enslaved to false worship.

The Old Testament church became more and more idolatrous, so that by the time of Samson's ministry, the people were unconcerned about the spiritual state of the church. Every man was doing what was right in his own eyes, just like every man today wants to be in control of the world around him. If people ignore God's law, written or natural, and desire to be a law unto themselves, their way of life (culture) becomes destructive. Individualism turns into anarchy. This principle applies to the church or the culture. It is a universal principle taught in Scripture.

The principle of confederation and the principle of monarchy did not find much favor with God's people during the Judges. Israel was a troubled confederacy! In the past when the children of Israel did evil in the sight of the Lord, they quickly cried out to the Lord for help and deliverance. However, now the Bible tells us that they simply did evil in the sight of the Lord. The previous generations cried for help, but now the Israelites had grown accustomed to being a slave to the foreign gods. The Israelites had no desire to call on the true and living God for deliverance. They were comfortable and adaptable to "whatever." The Old Testament church accommodated the false gods of the ungodly culture.

The church in every generation tends to accommodate the culture rather than being an instrument of reformation for culture. Any ungodly culture will try to change the church into a more accommodating organization. How is this accomplished? The culture says to the professing Christian, "follow me and you will be like God." Every generation becomes raptured into a state of ecstasy and falls into the trap of cultural accommodation. The church becomes enslaved by the ideas and fashions of men; the culture devours the church as a beast devours its prey. An example of being "raptured into a state of ecstasy," is the shift from the pastor being a shepherd for the congregation (Acts 20:28) to the pastor who is like a chief executive officer of a corporation. The culture has convinced the church that bureaucratic mangers are more important that godly elders watching over the flock. The church has followed the culture with psychological manipulations to sooth the heartache of a sinful soul. The manipulative ideas of an ungodly culture are charming and appealing, unless the Word of God is held forth as the ultimate means to determine the doctrine and practice of the church.

The New Testament church is a troubled confederacy because the visible church is fragmented into a thousand pieces, so that no real confederation exists. Some churches may be joined together (confederated) in principle, but not in practice.

The life and ministry of Samson is similar in some sense, but much different in other ways from the previous judges. The similarities are common among sinful people and the differences are merely contrasts rather than comparisons. The birth of Samson was unique, but we should not glamorize or spiritualize this event. Using allegory to interpret the life of Samson will follow the path of hero worship. The story of Samson's life is the story of a man that accommodated the culture.

The parents of Samson had received a noble calling, but who would think that they would go down in biblical history as very important people. Manoah was a man of whom we know very little. He was from the tribe of Dan and the tribe of Dan did not have a very good reputation. That is not to say that Manoah was like the devilish Danites, but then again Manoah was in the wrong crowd. Samson's parents made a good start. They sought advice from the angel as to, "what the boy's rule of life would be and his work" (Judges 13:12). Can you imagine anyone going to the Lord and asking the question: "How should I train my child for life and work?" Where should parents who love God go for advice on the rules of life for their children? Should parents consult the ungodly media of the day, friends, ungodly psychological books, unsaved relatives, public schools or a university? The answer to that question is no for all those resources. Manoah went to the nearest thing to the Word of the Lord, he went to the angel of the Lord. The Bible is the primary source of life training for children.

Manoah was diligent in his inquiry. His wife had already been informed of their responsibilities, but Manoah wanted to hear it for himself. If the Bible does not instruct the spiritual head of the home about his children then the parents mock God's instruction, for the Word of God instructs parents to, "train up a child in the way he shall go And when he is old he will not depart from it" (Proverbs 22:6).

The instructions Samson's parents received from the angel of the Lord would not be pleasing to the ears of most parents. The angel instructed Samson's parents to dedicate the boy to a perpetual Nazirite vow. The Nazirite vow stipulated three requirements.

1. Abstain from the fruit of the vine (wine, not even grapes).

2. No cutting of the hair.

3. Do not come into the presence of a dead body.

Today a person would consider it odd for making such a vow. The Nazirite vow does not require anything that one is incapable of doing. However, some churches require church leaders to take a vow of sexual virginity, which is something that most humans are incapable of doing. For example, if some of the church leaders in the Roman Catholic Church are required to take a vow of clerical celibacy, they vow to remain unmarried and restrain from any sexual thoughts or behavior. Since a vow cannot be broken, any sexual thoughts, sexual passions or sexual activity is a sin against God. I bring this to the attention of readers to clarify that making a Nazirite vow did not violate the will of man. Did Samson's vow refer to a long-haired teetotaler who could not visit a funeral parlor? The answer is no! Those outward signs symbolized subjection to the Lord. If a person was incapable of obeying those three rules, it would be impossible to faithfully obey the Lord. Apparently, during the period of the Old Testament, God used the Nazirite doctrine to demonstrate covenant faithfulness.

God speaking through the prophet Amos said, "I raised up some of your sons as prophets, and some of your young men as Nazirites" (Amos 2:11). God always has a remnant of leaders and laymen who are faithful to the Lord. For example, during the 4th century A.D., the church was debating the doctrine of the Trinity. The church was divided over whether Christ was like God the Father or of "one substance with the Father" (*The Nicene Creed*, 325 A.D.). Arianism taught that the Son was similar to the Father, but not the same substance with the Father. "An observer in that day might well have thought Arianism was going to triumph in the church" (*Evangelical Dictionary of Theology,* ed. Walter A. Elwell, p. 75). Obviously, the church survived. In the 16th century, John Calvin was distressed over the pastoral leadership in the church. "So it turns out that their [pastors] discourses possess no more truth and seriousness than if a player were acting out a tale on the stage" (*Concerning Scandals*, by John Calvin, p. 70). The church has been troubled from within and without for every generation. The church has always had internal as well as external enemies.

However, God has a remnant to fulfill the purpose, mission, and ministry of the church.

The state of Israel during the period of the Judges can only be described in terms of decline and disorder. The religious cult and the theocratic state were destitute of any monarchical rule. Their spiritual worship and secular culture was ruled by individual, ungodly, preferences. However, their lives were not unlike the church and culture of this age. They abandoned the principle of confederacy. Samson's exploits are always independent. The Bible does not indicate any reference to Samson seeking the counsel, advice, and assistance from anyone.

It appears that Samson wanted to be independent. It is a colossal error to think that man is an independent being. God alone is independent. It takes a man abounding in pride and arrogance to take on the whole world single-handed. Samson always acted alone. He did not seek help from the tribes of Israel. There was no confederation among the people. In the New Testament, it is called the communion of saints. The New Testament teaches that Christians are supposed to have fellowship with one another (1 Corinthians 1:9). The reciprocal commands in the New Testament such as love one another, encourage one another, and serve one another require a confederation to accomplish the commands.

The period of the Judges reminds me of the present state of the church and the majority of western culture. Complacency is an enemy to God's people. When professing Christians are satisfied with religious belief, no matter how broad and watered down, there will be trauma in the church. The tyranny of the power mongers in both church and culture diminishes the virtue of integrity. Even more frightening are those who seek absolute power over the people of this nation. However, my confidence is in the Lord. I remember a sermon by Dr. R. G. Lee entitled "Payday Is Someday." The Lord will separate the chaff from the wheat and separate the sheep from the goats. He will return!

The church has been seduced by Satan's lies. Then, the postmodern culture charms professing Christians with deceptive statements like, "absolute objective truth is not necessary for cultural civility." According to Richard Tarnas, the postmodernist states, "the nature of truth and reality, in science no less than in philosophy, religion, or art, is radically ambiguous" (The *Passion of the Western Mind*, by Richard Tarnas, p. 397). The church stands Silent in the midst of an ever-darkening culture.

Many evangelicals cry in a loud voice, "love one another." Although "love one another," is a commandment from the mouth of God, He also commands His children to maintain generational continuity of biblical doctrine. Teaching sound biblical doctrine is an act of love. Under inspiration of the Holy Spirit Paul the apostle said, "the things that you have heard from me among many witnesses, commit these to faithful men who will able to teach others" (2 Timothy 2:2), which refers to the generation to come. Those who went before Samson apparently had little concern for leaving any godly enduring principles. Each generation gave up some portion of Joshua's commandment from the Lord which was, "serve the Lord in sincerity and truth" (Joshua 24:14). Nearly 300 years before the time of Samson the people promised to put away the foreign gods. However, they did not keep the promise. Even worse, they passed on the foreign gods to each generation.

Fourteen hundred years after the time of the Judges, Paul the apostle went to the Greek city of Athens. While he was in Athens, Paul went to the "market place every day with those who happened to be present" (Acts 17:17). Even though hundreds of years had passed since the golden era at Athens, it was still the intellectual center for that part of the world. The market place was the center of public activity in

111

Athens. It was the place that philosophers would dialogue on subject's like wisdom and life. It was the place that people went to discuss subjects of interest or to hear the latest news. As the culture of Athens tried to make sense out of life, Paul observed two distinguishing features about the Athenian culture. First, Paul observed they were "very religious." Then he concluded they worshipped many gods even, "TO THE UNKNOWN GOD."

Aristides, the philosopher of Athens, around 125 A.D. made a defense before Hadrian the King on behalf of reverence for God.

> For it is clear to us, O King, that there are three classes of men in this world; these being the worshippers of the gods acknowledged among you, and Jews, and Christians. Further they who pay homage to many gods are themselves divided into three classes, Chaldeans namely, and Greeks, and Egyptians; for these have been guides and preceptors to the rest of the nations in the service and worship of these many-titled deities. (*Post-Nicene Fathers, The Apology of Aristides*, Vol. 10, Section 2)

The most powerful nations influenced the lesser nations with many titled deities. The most powerful culture influences the lesser culture. I understand why unbelievers worship many titled deities, (false gods) in this age, but I do not understand why Christians remain so cozy with the false gods. Why is there so much silence, when there should be so much noise detesting and resisting the wickedness that prevails in this country. Like Samson, many professing Christians and evangelical churches are influenced by many titled deities. The land is filled with people like Samson who have turned the worship of God into a mockery. People, material objects, concepts and institutions are titled deities that may replace the one true and living God. It may be Hollywood celebrities, the entertainment industry, sports events, hobbies, civic clubs, food, real estate are a few of the many titled deities.

Whether God worked in the soul of Samson so that Samson's mind and will changed according to God's Word by His Spirit, I cannot say. You can be assured that either God works in men to change their minds and wills or God works through men to accomplish His purpose without changing their minds or wills. The Bible does teach that the Spirit of God "came upon many of the judges." That does not mean they were necessarily the elect of God. The Spirit of God came upon King Saul, but the Bible also says the Spirit left Saul. It is not our responsibility to determine the eternal destiny of these judges or any other human being. It is our responsibility to "hold fast the pattern of sound words" as we find them in Scripture and pass them to the next generation. If God works through us without working in us, we may end up in the age of Samson or to put it in familiar terms the age when every man does what is right in his own eyes.

Although Samson was a man of faith, he accommodated the pagan culture and gave up his role as a spiritual leader. God called Samson to the role of a Nazirite, a spiritual leader, but Samson's life was not representative of a faithful Nazirite. Samson loved the secular culture rather than the sacred congregation. Samson passionately sought intermarriage with a Philistine woman, which was prohibited by Scripture. Samson had a passion for a heathen wife, and his parents arranged and participated in the wickedness. Mixed marriages in Israel were the mark of the downfall of that society. Mixed marriages were not uncommon throughout the history of Israel (Nehemiah 13:23-27). Samson's worldview was man-centered and focused on self-glory and self-satisfaction. "It's all about me" was rampant back in the time of the Judges, as today!

Samson looked for happiness and fulfillment from an ungodly culture. He accommodated the ungodly culture by seeking alliances apart from those who are in a covenant relationship with God. He lived under the influence of a wicked government. He forgot a fundamental principle, "The heart is deceitful above all things, and desperately wicked (Jeremiah 17:9).

Since human eyes are corrupted eyes, they tend not to want to look into the face of God. The human mouth attached to those human eyes may easily say, "my purpose is to glorify and enjoy God," but then those same eyes and that same mouth may be more inclined to glorify and enjoy an ungodly culture.

Return to the Lord, seek His face, speak His words and influence the ungodly culture.

12. Religious Culture

Now there was a man from the mountains of Ephraim, whose name was Micah. And he said to his mother, "The eleven hundred shekels of silver that were taken from you, and on which you put a curse, even saying it in my ears—here is the silver with me; I took it." And his mother said, "May you be blessed by the LORD, my son!" So when he had returned the eleven hundred shekels of silver to his mother, his mother said, "I had wholly dedicated the silver from my hand to the LORD for my son, to make a carved image and a molded image; now therefore, I will return it to you." Thus he returned the silver to his mother. Then his mother took two hundred shekels of silver and gave them to the silversmith, and he made it into a carved image and a molded image; and they were in the house of Micah. The man Micah had a shrine, and made an ephod and household idols; and he consecrated one of his sons, who became his priest. In those days there was no king in Israel; everyone did what was right in his own eyes. Now there was a young man from Bethlehem in Judah, of the family of Judah; he was a Levite, and was staying there. The man departed from the city of Bethlehem in Judah to stay wherever he could find a place. Then he came to the mountains of Ephraim, to the house of Micah, as he journeyed. And Micah said to him, "Where do you come from?" So he said to him, "I am a Levite from Bethlehem in Judah, and I am on my way to find a place to stay." Micah said to him, "Dwell with me, and be a father and a priest to me, and I will give you ten shekels of silver per year, a suit of clothes, and your sustenance." So the Levite went in. Then the Levite was content to dwell with the man; and the young man became like one of his sons to him. So Micah consecrated the Levite, and the young man became his priest, and lived in the house of Micah. Then Micah said, "Now I know that the LORD will be good to me, since I have a Levite as priest!"

Judges 17:1-13

A friend introduced me to a man I did not know. My friend said, "Mr. such & such, this is my pastor, Martin Murphy." The man looked at me with piercing, penetrating eyes and said, "I'm not a religious man." The question that came to my mind without making it vocal was, "how does a person live in a religious culture without being religious?" To avoid a ruckus I did not tell him that everyone is religious.

Judges chapter seventeen describes the religious, political, and social condition in Israel throughout the period of the Judges. God's people had ignored the fundamental principles, which should have brought peace rather than oppression. It was a troubled culture, but a very religious culture. Our focus as Christians must be on the religious life in our culture. The dominant culture in the land of promise was ungodly. If religious life is out of control, you can be assured that every other aspect of life will be in a state of chaos.

The opening words of Judges chapter seventeen sound like a child's storybook. It begins with, "now there was a man from the mountains of Ephraim whose name was Micah." We might use a little different language with our children, something like this, "Once upon a time there was a man named Micah. . ." There is no mention of apostasy in Israel, no oppression in Israel, and no mention of a Judge for Israel. What is noticeable during the period of the Judges is the inescapable relativism in those days when there was no king in Israel and every man did what was right in his own eyes.

I have heard preachers call the period of the judges a time of anarchy, but that is not exactly true. Anarchy means no rule. A careful study of the Book of Judges reveals there were periodic times of peace and then there were times of apostasy and chaos. Israel abandoned the principle of confederation and the principle of monarchy. However, that does not necessarily translate into anarchy.

The political and religious condition in the United States at the beginning of the 21st century is probably similar to the Israelites during the period of the Judges. To a greater or lesser degree, they experienced civil tyranny and spiritual apostasy. During the early period of the Judges, the tyranny and apostasy was local and occasional, then later on, it was universal and persistent.

The story in Judges Chapter seventeen is about a layman named Micah who lived in the hill country of Ephraim and a Levite (a priest) who had been living in Jerusalem. Although Micah was a professing child of God, his life did not represent the child of the King. It is almost like a story found in a tabloid newspaper at the check out counter in grocery stores.

Micah was a thief but not just a regular old thief. He stole from his own mother. He confessed his sin because his mother called down a curse on the one who stole all her silver. Fear got the best of him and he returned the silver back to his mother. Micah was a thief whose mother neither chastises him nor warns him of his sin, but puts her stamp of approval on him by making an idol for his shrine. Micah had a shrine or as the Hebrew text literally says, "a house of gods" (Judges 17:5). Obviously, this new image was honored among Micah's idols in his personal shrine. Had Micah forgotten or had he never known what the Lord had told Moses when the people of Israel built the golden calf? Micah was like many religious people who think more highly of themselves than they should. He determined to worship according to his personal pleasure, even if it was contrary to the teaching of Scripture.

Micah worshipped many gods. Apparently, he ignored God's instruction for worship. "An altar of earth you shall make for Me, and you shall sacrifice on it your burnt offerings and your peace offerings, your sheep and your oxen? In every place where I Record My name I will come to you, and I will bless you." (Exodus 20:24). However, Micah thinks his way is the best way to find satisfaction in worship, even though God had said otherwise. If Micah were alive today, he might say something like, "I like contemporary lively worship. I know what the Bible says, but..." and then try to explain away the Word of God.

Micah placed too high a price on his personal place of worship. In the modern church as in the days of Micah, too much emphasis has been placed on buildings. God has no interest in buildings or personal shrines. Christians gather to worship God, not because of the building, but because of the presence of the Lord. Sometimes buildings become idols and then sometimes the contents in the buildings become idols. These are signs of a very religious culture.

Micah had every religious idea and concept known to him all mixed together and he worshiped idols. After his sin against his mother and all his gross sin against God, Micah hired his own son to be a priest. Why did Micah appoint his son a priest even when the law of God prohibited it? The most likely reason is that Micah was a very religious person. Maybe he could not find a priest that would be faithful to Micah and his many gods. I am not sure and neither does anyone else know if there was any organized priesthood in Israel at the time. There is one thing we know for sure. Religious life in Israel during the time of the Judges was nothing more than privatized religion. This is the crux of a disoriented church. "Every man does what is right in his own eyes." One man in the church wants to do one thing and another wants to do something else, but there is no king in the church. The church abandons the monarchial principle by ignoring God's instruction.

Micah was so messed up that he eventually hired a Levite to be his own private preacher. Now, if you think that the present day church has not stooped that low, you are wrong. What we have here is one man, Micah (a name that might fit any person in the contemporary church) who wants a blessing from God, so he hires his own preacher. Micah thought he owned the preacher. The contemporary church is filled with people who think they own the preacher.

The story in Judges is a reminder of the condition of the church today. Preachers find themselves ministering to people who want to make the preacher conform to their personal standards. It is an absolute abandonment of the monarchial principle. However, part of the blame is at the preacher's doorstep. Many preachers simply follow the Levite mandate and justify it with man-made religion. "Then the Levite was content to dwell with the man" (Judges 17:11). The Levite was content to be a priest among the sinful idolatries of Micah. The Levite was content with a poor salary in comparison with the way God had made provision for the Levites.

Micah represents the people in the pews of the church. Unfortunately, Micah did not understand the monarchial principle and that gave him a sense of false assurance. The Levite represents the pulpit in the church. Furthermore, the Levite did not understand his responsibilities as the spiritual leader of God's people.

The prevailing attitude in the church today is the same wicked attitude that prevailed during the period of the Judges. "Every man did what was right in his own eyes." This style of wicked democracy has plagued the church and the North American culture for too many centuries. The church will have a positive influence on culture, if it does what is right in God's eyes. Attending a religious meeting in a building, commonly known as "the church" will not bring the blessing of God. Micah hired a personal priest. Micah said, "Now I know that the Lord will be good to me, since I have a Levite as priest" (Judges 17:13). Micah was very religious and like many professing Christians engaged in religious activity, but that will not secure the blessing of God. There is only one way to secure the blessing of God and that is for the true and living God to call you to Himself by the power of His Spirit through the finished work of His Son, the Lord Jesus Christ.

Much of the religious life in the United States at the beginning of the 21st century, as in the days of Judges, is according to human inventions. With the exception of true nihilism, the principle that nothing exists in reality, all people believe in "being" rather than "non-being." At the very least, religion is the belief and practice of something transcendental with eternal effects.

Paul appeared before Felix, a Roman governor, because the Jews charged Paul with breaking Jewish law. Felix turned the case over to King Agrippa and explained that the Jews "had some question against him [Paul] about their own religion" (Acts 25:19). The Jews had their religion, the Romans had their religion and Christians had their religion. Everybody had a religion. Not all religions are equal and not all religions will secure a favorable relationship with God.

Culture and religion intermingle because together they define a way of life. Culture, generally speaking, refers to the secular dimension of life. Religion, generally speaking, refers to the sacred dimension of life. The Roman Catholic theologian, Hans Küng, alludes to paradigms of society and religion. Although distinct, culture and religion have some agreement.

> Religion, therefore, does not simply pass on more or less self-evident, universal convictions, values, and behavior patterns of an epoch. In religion...a comprehensive meaning of life is conveyed, the highest ideals and unconditional norms are proclaimed and guaranteed, and a final spiritual homeland and community is offered to believers. (*Theology for the Third Millennium*, by Hans Küng, p. 212)

In the 14th century B.C., Micah allowed the culture to captivate his mind. The dominant culture in the 21st century captivates Christian minds at an alarming rate.

Robert Burton's *The Anatomy of Melancholy*, analyzes the causes and cures of melancholy, covering a vast scope of scholarship in numerous fields, such as classical studies, theology, philosophy, science, and politics. In his notable work, Burton said, "One religion is as true as another." Religion is a curiosity among human beings. It is because religion is about what people believe and practice.

Men and women are passionate about what they believe about religion. If it is man-made religion, it is false and secular. God is passionate about what He believes, however His belief system is true and sacred. Man-made religion is temporary and God-made religion is eternal. If there are two belief systems, then there are two religions. If one is man-made religion and the other is God-made religion, they will be in conflict.

The term "man-made religion" refers to religious practices that result from man's ideas rather than God's Word. Jesus exposed the man-made religion of the Pharisees, the conservatives among the Jewish leaders. The gospel of Luke summarizes a meeting Jesus had with a Pharisee. The Pharisee invited Jesus for dinner, but Jesus did not participate in a ceremonial washing before the meal.

> When the Pharisee saw it, he marveled that He had not first washed before dinner. Then the Lord said to him, "Now you Pharisees make the outside of the cup and dish clean, but your inward part is full of greed and wickedness. Foolish ones! Did not He who made the outside make the inside also? But rather give alms of such things as you have; then indeed all things are clean to you. But woe to you Pharisees! For you tithe mint and rue and all manner of herbs,

and pass by justice and the love of God. These you ought to have done, without leaving the others undone." (Luke 11:38-42)

The Pharisees allegedly followed the law of Moses. The law required God's people to give, "All the tithe of the land, whether of the seed of the land or of the fruit of the tree is the Lord's" (Leviticus 27:30). However, the religious leaders had distorted the Word of God. According to the *Mishnah* (oral interpretation of the Law by Jewish leaders), the herb "rue" was exempt from the tithe. They not only distorted the Word of God, it was a regular habit for them. Luke used the Greek word translated "tithe" in the present tense and active voice. It describes "tithing" rue as a continuous action, thus a continual distortion of the Word of God. The Pharisees did not understand the Word of God and they were not explaining it correctly. They distorted the Word of God and turned it into man-made religion. Many churches continue the tradition of past years without inquiry into the truthfulness of the interpretation, like those of the Jewish tradition.

There are many ways of turning the Word of God into man-made religion. For instance, some liberal theologians teach that the resurrection of Christ was merely a spiritual resurrection. "[Wolfhart] Pannenberg argues against a corporeal resurrection body [of Jesus Christ] in favor of appearances which are described in terms of a spiritual body which was recognized as Jesus..." (*Evangelical Dictionary of Theology, edited by Walter Elwell*, p. 940). From the extreme man-made religion that denies the physical resurrection of Jesus Christ to the less significant man-made religious activities, they originate in the cultural milieu.

The Christian religion will never be completely pure from every stain, but if there is any purity at all, it will be the result of our understanding the Word of God. A survey of the history of the people of God in the Old Testament reveals suffering because the Word of God was not their standard for faith and worship. The dominant false religion of the culture in the land of promise captivated God's people so they turned away from true religion.

God has given His church true religion. The precepts are found in the Word of God. The practice of true religion is to engage in the culture with the gifts and abilities from God. To use those gifts properly, one must "act justly and to love mercy, and to walk humbly with your God" (Micah 6:8). To act justly means to think, speak, and act fairly and honestly towards God and men. Heavy-handed treatment and dishonesty is the product of man-made religion. It will eventually find its way to the surface and if taken too far it will create a cultural disaster. To love mercy means to show kindness by forgiving and reconciling when relationships fall apart. Walk humbly with God means to have a constant sense of your sin before you.

Walking humbly with God means to have a sense of God's holiness before you. To walk humbly with God means to recognize your weakness and God's power. To walk humbly with God means to acknowledge the saving grace of God in your prosperity and in your adversity.

A religious culture without Christ may charm the professing believer. A snake may charm you, but remember its bite may be poisonous. A religious culture with Christ may challenge the professing believer. The challenge is never beyond your reach because God's grace is great.

13. Generational Continuity

In those days there was no king in Israel. And in those days the tribe of the Danites was seeking an inheritance for itself to dwell in; for until that day their inheritance among the tribes of Israel had not fallen to them. So the children of Dan sent five men of their family from their territory, men of valor from Zorah and Eshtaol, to spy out the land and search it. They said to them, "Go, search the land." So they went to the mountains of Ephraim, to the house of Micah, and lodged there. While they were at the house of Micah, they recognized the voice of the young Levite. They turned aside and said to him, "Who brought you here? What are you doing in this place? What do you have here?" He said to them, "Thus and so Micah did for me. He has hired me, and I have become his priest." So they said to him, "Please inquire of God, that we may know whether the journey on which we go will be prosperous." And the priest said to them, "Go in peace. The presence of the LORD be with you on your way." So the five men departed and went to Laish. They saw the people who were there, how they dwelt safely, in the manner of the Sidonians, quiet and secure. There were no rulers in the land who might put them to shame for anything. They were far from the Sidonians, and they had no ties with anyone.

Judges 18:1-7

Generational continuity will prevail until there is a change or a collapse. Generational continuity may be good or bad, depending on the model that each generation has to follow. The question may be asked, "How did previous generations err to the point that the culture is ready to collapse." Dr. Harold Parker explains a universal principle.

The tendency [is] for the student to follow the authority ahead of him in Indian file, deeper and deeper into the morass of error. If the first of the secondary authorities is wrong in fact or judgment, then all who follow him will be in error also, for they are on the same path. They will remain in error until the primary sources are checked again" (*Studies in Southern Presbyterian History*, by Dr. Harold Parker, p. 56).

Dr. Parker was a church historian and in his book, he traced the history and development of Southern Presbyterian churches during the middle of the 19th century. At one point, Dr. Parker asked the question, "How then can the testimony of so many church historians be in error?" One reason according to Dr. Parker is, "few historians seemingly have taken the pains to work through a church union from its original basis for union."

The clarion call for the Italian Renaissance (1350 A.D. – 1425 A.D.) was the Latin phrase *ad fontes*. It literally means, "to the sources." It was a call to return to the classics and writings of the ancient Greek and Roman literature. For Christians of every generation, the war cry ought to be "return to the original sources."

When Dr. Parker referred to the historians passing on error, it is an apt analogy of Christians passing on to the next generation principles and practice. The principles will be right or wrong, but the only way to know is to return to the sources, (*ad fontes*). For instance, the first principle for Christians is to worship God. Therefore, Christians must be the church rather than practice "going to the church." The principle is right, but the practice is wrong. Return to the source to recover the truth. The Word that God the Holy Spirit chose to use to describe His church is the Greek word *ekklesia*, which literally translated means, "called out." Christians who return to the source, the Bible, will discover that the church is the people of God. It is not a building, an organization, or a place. It is the congregation of God's people. The church assembles to worship, receive instruction, fellowship, and pray. If someone instructs a child to get ready to go to church and to be quiet in church, the child will naturally grow up with the idea that the building or the organization he or she is associated with is the church. If he or she does not return to the source and discover that the church is "the people of God," he or she may, to some degree, come to worship the building or some of the tangible assets that God provided for His people. Untold numbers of professing Christians have suffered because of disputes over property, furniture, and assets, because they have been taught that those things are the church, and it is their duty to protect the church.

The text in Judges reveals inspired principles for the modern church. One distinctive factor stands out and may apply to any future generation. "In those days there was no king in Israel" (Judges 18:1). There was no godly biblical leadership in the church. Also, "There were no rulers in the land" (Judges 18:7). Therefore, the culture was in a state of anarchy.

The word anarchy derives from two Greek words, *an* is a negation which may be translated "without" and *archon* which refers to a "leader" thus, no leader. Anarchy does not just happen. It requires effort to eliminate a good orderly government and dismiss proper rule in the land. Strange as it may sound, anarchy follows democracy. Democracy is the collective rule of the majority of the people in a given society. The word democracy comes from two Greek words, *demos* which means "people" and *arche* which means "rule." It sound a bit crass but pure democracy is mob rule.

The passion of political democracy is derived from philosophical individualism. Since the sin of Adam, it is inherent in the human race to desire to be in control. It is called individual autonomy. Autonomy derives from two Greek words, *autos* which refers to "self" and *nomos* which refers to "law". The autonomous man believes he has ultimate authority. The autonomous man says, "I am and there is no one else besides me" (Isaiah 47:10). Sinful autonomy is the cause of individualism. The reason everyone does what seems right in his own eyes may be traced to the Garden of Eden. It seemed right in Eve's eyes to follow the charm of Satan, the leader of autonomy and individualism.

God has given His people the biblical principle of confederation and the biblical principle of monarchy. The principle of confederation states that people join together for a common purpose. The civil dimension of life functions best when God's people associate and cooperate in their social, political, cultural, and economic lives for the glory of God. In the New Testament, the confederation concept is described as a partnership. The theological terminology is the communion of the saints. The idea is participation and sharing together in the work and blessings of the kingdom of God. (See Philippians 1:5).

As a nation, the United States has abandoned the biblical principle of confederation and adopted the unbiblical principle of democracy. The cultural elites charm the people with the idea that there is a collective democracy when in fact the people have very little if any authority in the ultimate rule of the society. Instead, there is centralized power, multiculturalism, and despotism regulating the individuals of the society. Centralized power belongs only to the triune God. Multiculturism is not a biblical principle. God divided men into different people groups because of sin and man has not perfected himself. Despotism results when one or just a few people hold centralized power. Ungodly despotism is sinful and anti-biblical.

The biblical principle of monarchy refers to God's rule over His people according to his word. There is one theological and moral belief system and it is found in the Word of God. As a church, we have abandoned the biblical principle of monarchy and adopted the unbiblical principle of democracy for the church. There is no democracy with truth. God is the absolute monarch who reveals the truth in His Word.

If sinful man claims to have ultimate authority, the result is individualism and individualism leads to anarchy. England has suffered from the conflict of opposing cultures in recent history. One worldview calls for a Judeo/Christian ethic. The other world view calls for human autonomy and everyone doing what is right in his or her own eyes (individualism). I believe the current worldview in England is a result of the enculturation of the British Empire. They tried to assimilate every culture into one under the rule of the monarch. It is an unbiblical principle.

A brief survey of Genesis Chapter eleven reveals that, "the Lord confused the language of all the earth and from there the Lord scattered them abroad over the face of all the earth" (Genesis 11:9).

Christians ought to analyze their inheritance and ask the question, "was it a good or bad model for living according to a Christian culture?" If the model is like Judges chapter eighteen, and everyone is doing what is right in his or her own eyes, it is bad. If the model is like Psalm 97:1 and "The Lord reigns" it is good. Either way, generational continuity will have its effect.

Judges chapter eighteen is the historical account of the Danites. The tribe of Dan was the last tribe of Israel to receive its portion of the Promised Land. Their portion was not very accommodating. They were squeezed between Judah to the South, Ehpriam to the north, Benjamin to the east and the Mediterranean Sea to the west. For whatever reasons, the tribe of Dan did not consider their inheritance sufficient for their needs. "Therefore, the Danites were seeking an inheritance for themselves to dwell" (Judges 18:1). They sent spies to find a suitable place to settle. During the trip, the spies ended up visiting at the place Micah lived. The spies finally located the place they would settle. It was to the north of all the tribes in a little place called Laish. The Laishians were anarchists and separatists. They were violating two basic principles that will ultimately bring destruction. The first principle is for the leader of any culture, organization, society, or church to rule according to righteousness and justice (See Psalm 97:1-2). The Laishians violated this principle because, "there were no rulers in the land" (Judges 18:7). The second principle is to secure the land by confederating with like-minded people (See 2 Samuel 10:17-19. The Laishians violated this principle because, "they had no ties with anyone" (Judges 18:7). There was no restraint against the wickedness in the land. There was an absence of authority in both the state and the church. Furthermore, there was an absence of authority in Israel as well as heathen nations such as Laish.

With the principles cast aside, the men from the tribe of Dan went to Micah's house, stole his household gods, took his priest, and went merrily away. They destroyed the people of Laish and established their new home. To make matters worse, the Danites (the people of God), "set up for themselves Micah's carved image" (Judges 18:31). They disobeyed the Word of God, because God commanded them to worship at Shiloh. The tribe of Dan represented the people of God, but Dan was a bad model and look at what happened to the generations that followed them. The tribe of Dan became a monument of wickedness, even though outwardly they called themselves the church. Eventually the Assyrians destroyed them. The culture consumed the church, just like the culture in the Garden of Eden (Satan) consumed the church (Adam and Eve). Each generation has its own particular enemies, but the principles from the Word of God are the same for every generation.

The belief system and actions of every professing Christian will have an effect on the next generation. Therefore, every Christian ought to return to the sources to make sure that their faith and actions are consistent with the Word of God. You think, act, and believe like you do because of the Spirit of God in you or the lack of it and what has been passed on to you by the previous generation.

What kind of church did the previous generation leave this present generation? Was it a good model or was it a bad model? When applied personally, you will have to answer that for yourself. When applied to the church we have church history to answer the question. It is certain that Scripture and church history reveals that many souls inherited a bad model.

The once strong evangelical church in the United States stands on the precipice of a neo-dark age. The culture charms the church. The church is aware that the civil affairs in the United States are disenfranchised from any kind of biblical ethic. The church is also aware that religious affairs are void of the absolute authority from the Word of God. God's people may say, "I know what the Bible says but..." however it is rebellion against or rejection of the authority of Scripture.

If Jesus Christ is your Lord, surely you want to leave a good model for the next generation. Make every effort to learn and apply the biblical principles of confederation and monarchy. Do not let the wickedness of previous generations lead you down a dark path. Believe, acknowledge, and act like Jesus Christ is the King of kings. Sound the alarm to return to the sources, *ad fontes.*

Without reservation, Christians have every confidence that Jesus Christ is the King of kings. He is the great monarch of all earthly kingdoms. Jesus Christ is the King of His church and He will return for Her on the last day.

14. Cultural Decadence

As they were enjoying themselves, suddenly certain men of the city, perverted men, surrounded the house and beat on the door. They spoke to the master of the house, the old man, saying, "Bring out the man who came to your house, that we may know him carnally!" But the man, the master of the house, went out to them and said to them, "No, my brethren! I beg you, do not act so wickedly! Seeing this man has come into my house, do not commit this outrage. Look, here is my virgin daughter and the man's concubine; let me bring them out now. Humble them, and do with them as you please; but to this man do not do such a vile thing!" But the men would not heed him. So the man took his concubine and brought her out to them. And they knew her and abused her all night until morning; and when the day began to break, they let her go. Then the woman came as the day was dawning, and fell down at the door of the man's house where her master was, till it was light. When her master arose in the morning, and opened the doors of the house and went out to go his way, there was his concubine, fallen at the door of the house with her hands on the threshold. And he said to her, "Get up and let us be going." But there was no answer. So the man lifted her onto the donkey; and the man got up and went to his place. When he entered his house he took a knife, laid hold of his concubine, and divided her into twelve pieces, limb by limb, and sent her throughout all the territory of Israel. And so it was that all who saw it said, "No such deed has been done or seen from the day that the children of Israel came up from the land of Egypt until this day. Consider it, confer, and speak up!"

Judges 19: 22-30

The deterioration of a secular culture is certain if society fails to follow the godly principles from the Word of God. The Old Testament church during the time of the Judges was in possession of God's principles, but they chose to ignore them. Confusion was rampant in Israel. The people of God rejected God as their King (the principle of monarchy), so the writer of Judges said, "In these days there was no king in Israel" (Judges 17:6) The culture had no common purpose, so the writer of Judges said, "everyone did what was right in his own eyes" (Judges 17:6).

The events in Chapter 19 of the Book of Judges summarize the cultural decadence of God's people. It is the descriptive history of God's people living in a godless culture. The insanity of a godless culture, evident during the time of the Judges, is apparent in most of western civilization at the beginning of the 21st century.

The story begins by describing the circumstances of a priest from Ephraim taking a woman to be his concubine. There are several reasons to believe that this woman was his wife. The priest is called "her husband" (Judges 19:3) and there is no mention of the priest having another wife. The woman ran away from her husband to live a sexually immoral life. She ended up living with her father. After a few months, the priest went to get his wife. On his way home, he stopped by the city of Gibeah to spend the night. If you can imagine a time when there were no motels and hotels, then you have described in your mind the culture of that day. In a covenant community, it would be expected, according to God's law, to give shelter and food to a traveler, especially one of God's covenant people. However, the Bible indicates, "no one took them into his home for the night." From this brief account, the depravity, self-centeredness, and thoughtlessness of a godless culture are evident. Finally, an old man invited the priest and his wife into his home supplying all their needs.

Now we come to the part of the story that is excruciatingly difficult. I will explain this plain enough for anyone to understand. Some men of the city wanted to have sex with the priest. After discussing the matter, the priest finally took his wife and gave her to the men. They raped and abused her throughout the night. The next morning the priest could not awaken her, because she was dead, so he threw her over the donkey and went home. This story describes the ungoverned culture during the time of Judges. Judges Chapter 19 is similar to the text in Genesis Chapter 19.

> Now the two angels came to Sodom in the evening, and Lot was sitting in the gate of Sodom. When Lot saw them, he rose to meet them, and he bowed himself with his face toward the ground. And he said, "Here now, my lords, please turn in to your servant's house and spend the night, and wash your feet; then you may rise early and go on your way. And they said, "No, but we will spend the night in the open square." But he insisted strongly; so they turned in to him and entered his house. Then he made them a feast, and baked unleavened bread, and they ate. Now before they lay down, the men of the city, the men of Sodom, both old and young, all the people from every quarter, surrounded the house. And they called to Lot and said to him, "Where are the men who came to you tonight? Bring them out to us that we may know them carnally." (Genesis 19:1-5)

The similarities of Sodom and Gibeah are striking. The history of those cultures reveals the moral decay eating away the fiber of society. However, there is one radical profound difference. The Sodomite culture was not regulated by God's Word, but the culture of Gibeah was regulated by God's Word. Something is seriously wrong when God's people cannot be distinguished from Satan's people.

The people of Israel were outraged over the wickedness at Gibeah. The gruesome story ends with a call to the tribes of Israel. The priest dissected his wife's body and sent each tribe a body part. The tribes were astonished and came to the same conclusion. "No such deed has been done or seen from the day that the children of Israel came up from the land of Egypt until this day. Consider it, confer, and speak up!" (Judges 19:30). The ungodly principles of the culture were revealed by the atrocious, despicable immorality. It was time for the Old Testament church to speak up and say as Joshua said, "choose for yourselves this day whom you will serve" (Joshua 24:15).

The church has a mandate to keep God's law. "Now therefore, if you will indeed obey My voice and keep my covenant, then you shall be a special treasure to Me above all people..." (Exodus 19:5). The covenant mentioned in Exodus chapter nineteen, that God made with His people, is commonly known as the Ten Commandments. Christians mistakenly blame God for pouring out His wrath on a person or a particular occasion, or a collective group of people. God does not pour out his wrath arbitrarily. God simply keeps his promise to punish those who break His law. Therefore, it is God's law that convicts the lawbreaker. God simply administers justice. However, the repentant child of God will find forgiveness, restoration, mercy, and saving grace because of Christ, the Mediator between God and man. The child of God does not demand justice, but rather pleads for mercy.

Since the culture has no Mediator, between sinful man and a holy God, obeying God's law is essential to maintain order, secure peace, and prevent chaos. The culture has an innate prompting to keep God's Law. The apostle Paul explains this universal and timeless principle to the church.

> For when Gentiles, who do not have the law, by nature do the things in the law, these, although not having the law, are a law to themselves, who show the work of the law written in their hearts, their conscience also bearing witness, and between themselves their thoughts accusing or else excusing them. (Romans 2:14-16)

Before sin entered the world, the law of God was a complete system of natural laws implanted in the hearts of men. The word "heart" is a metaphor for the soul of all rational creatures. God's law was implanted in the soul of Adam and Eve, Cain and Abel, Noah, his sons, Abram, and Joseph and all the people even though the law of God was not yet written in stone by the finger of God. All these men of old understood the law of God written on their souls.

The church and the culture have a God-given standard for ethical behavior. Even though the standard is the same, the motivation for obedience is different. The motivation for the child of God to obey the law is the love of God. The motivation for the unbeliever is self-preservation. One follows the principle of monarchy and dependence upon God the King. The other follows the principle of anarchy and independence from God.

God's people during the time of the Judges had God for their King. As their King, God had the right to and did make a covenant with them and all they had to do is obey God's voice. The sad state of Israel during the period of the judges was that those covenant people looked for justice from other men without seeking mercy from the Lord.

The perverted men from the tribe of Benjamin missed the mark, which is evident by their wickedness against the Levite and his wife (concubine). God's covenant demanded a civil and religious code of ethics, which they grossly violated. God's system of justice in the Old Covenant *was lex talionis* - an eye for an eye and a tooth for a tooth. The simple remedy was to execute those who committed the horrible crime. What followed is an example of how a society will quickly deteriorate into confusion and destruction. Such was the case with the tribe of Benjamin.

However, we should not be hasty to condemn the tribe of Benjamin. Although Benjamin turned away from the Lord, it was not the only tribe of Israel to miss the mark. Eventually the whole nation missed the mark. The history of the Old Testament church reveals their cultural decadence. From the Garden of Eden to the Babylonian captivity in 586 B.C., there were gross violations of God's law, just as we find in the book of Judges.

From the creation of the world to the urban populations of the modern western world, cultures come and go leaving behind a history of despair and defeat. However, with all the pretentious, uncivilized, and unethical behavior today, the time of the judges sounds like the present day culture.

The church has plagiarized the morality of the culture and syncretized religious worship to satisfy the culture. The church should stay on a straight course and should not turn to the right or the left. If the church turns to "pessimism," it may lead to despair. If the church turns to "optimism," it may lead to false hope. The pessimism in Israel led them to practice a most pernicious and dangerous sin. "Everyone did what was right in his own eyes." The optimism that leads to false hope is just as dangerous to Christians as pessimism that leads to despair. Just believing that everything will work out without putting our hands to the plough is foolish thinking.

When the Benjaminites ignored the warnings of the confederacy in Israel (the confederated tribes), obviously they were deceived by their own optimism. They did not think the Lord would demand justice through the hands of the other tribes of Israel.

We live in the world of reality. I fear that many Christians today are not willing to face reality. They are afraid of truth and do not know what to do with the truth when it stares them in the face. Christians are desperate to form a Christian sub-culture with unbiblical worldviews. They cherish feelings, intuition, experience, and illustrations rather than rational principles that may be devolved to future generations. There is so much strife, turmoil, and division in the visible church that its message of the law and gospel remains buried in the aftermath of internal fighting. As a church, we have the responsibility to be the salt of the earth and the light of the world during cultural chaos. The sad state of the church is that its membership refuses to acknowledge its rightful role in the society.

The church has come to the place where it wants to be like society, not a change agent to society. Has the church missed the mark? "Among all this people (the tribe of Benjamin) were seven hundred select men who were left-handed; every one could sling a stone at a hair's breadth and not miss" (Judges 20:16). How sad that these men who supposedly couldn't miss the mark, in the end, missed the mark.

15. Individualism Prevails

In those days there was no king in Israel; everyone did what was right in his own eyes.

Judges 21:25

The Book of Judges is an infallible account of the history of God's people from about the end of the conquest of Canaan by the Israelites until the monarchy was established in Israel. The Book of Judges has two parts. In the first part, Chapters 1-16, the author explains the chronological history of the development and the downfall of Israel.

In the second part, the author gives a narrative of two separate events. Chapters 17-18 describe religious worship in Israel during the whole period of the Judges. It is a story of a priest who sold his soul for a little money and some prestige. Chapters 19-21 describe the moral chaos in Israel during the period of the Judges.

It is likely that the author of Judges added these two stories at the end of his historical account to remind the reader of the instability of cult worship and the deterioration of the social order during the period of the Judges. I believe these were actual events that took place at various times during the period of the Judges. Chapters 19-21 are representative of the religious and social life during the whole period of the Judges.

The cultic anarchy described in chapters 17-18 and the social disorder found in chapters 19-21 are expressions of the oft-quoted theme statement: "In those days there was no king in Israel; everyone did what was right in his own eyes." Chapter 21 concludes the historical narrative on a sad note. The Israelites declared war on the tribe of Benjamin and as is typical of people, who neglect the principle of monarchy, they made rash and unreasonable vows, in order to gain God's favor. There is no reason to believe that the vows were necessary for the Israelites to have a victory.

The first vow was one that called for separatism. More specifically the tribes of Israel vowed not to allow any marriage to the Benjaminites. The second vow was one that called every Israelite man to war at the threat of death. Stated another way, if they did not come to fight against Benjamin, they would be put to death. After the war was over, the Israelites continued with their irrational senseless thinking. "Therefore they instructed the children of Benjamin saying, Go, lie in wait in the vineyards. And watch; and just when the daughters of Shiloh come out to perform their dances, then come out from the vineyards, and every man catch a wife for himself for the daughters of Shiloh; then go to the land of Benjamin" (Judges 21:20).

The Israelite elders not only carried out rash, ungodly vows, but then they used deceit and theft to keep from breaking their foolish vows. An irrational devious person will ultimately lie and steal to accomplish his own wicked purposes.

Behavior that produces that kind of mass confusion is senseless. It was present in the day of the Judges and remains with us until this day. Individualism is the worldview that produces irresponsible and mass confusion in the church and in the culture. Western culture is a hotbed of various worldviews like individualism, egalitarianism, statism, pragmatism, secularism, and many more. An individual person is a creative work of God. However, when the noun forming suffix, "ism," is added to the word "individual," it describes an ideology or a way of life. Individualism may become a false god to the individual. The state is a necessary component for social and political life. However, adding "ism" to the word, "state," may indicate that the state provides the means to save the individual belonging to the state. To put it another way, statism becomes a god to worship and the way of salvation for secular life. Egalitarian is a word that refers to equality in the human race. All humans are equal before God, because they are all sinful creatures. However, egalitarianism argues for equal rights economically, socially, politically, and culturally. All these worldviews especially, individualism, dominates the mind and scene of Evangelical Christianity, as well as the western culture.

There was a time when self-evident truths were held in high esteem in the American culture. At the same time, the church believed and taught that the Bible was absolute truth. General revelation to culture and special revelation to the church are the common threads that hold the fabric of life together. The denial of self-evident truths inclines the culture to do what is right in their own eyes. It is the denial of the inspired infallible truth of God's Word that inclines the church to agree with the culture. For those reasons, Christians should not be ignorant of the meaning of the final verse of the Book of Judges. "In those days there was no king in Israel; everyone did what was right in his own eyes."

This is the argument of the humanist. Individual man is the measure of all reality. It is nothing more than the old humanist argument of individual rights, which is a mere extension of the broader concept called individualism. During the time of the Judges, the most obvious dimension of individualism was the disregard for God's law and false worship. The state of affairs described by the author of Judges should get the attention of all professing believers. God's people were killing each other. During the three days of civil war among the tribes of Israel 65,000 men were killed. They refused to live under God's authority and 65,000 men died.

When the church ignores the authority of God, the culture will refuse to believe God has authority. There are professing believers who would endeavor to destroy the ministry of a church because of their individual preferences. While individualism is a chief enemy to the church, it is a favorite companion to the culture. The cultural historian, Richard Tarnas, accurately describes the underlying motive of the Western mind. "The great overriding impulse defining Western man since the Renaissance [is] the quest for independence, self-determination and individualism..." (*The Passion of the Western Mind*, by Richard Tarnas, p. 388).

The longer Christians insist on individualism to rule the church, the greater the cost will be in the end. Individualism is subjective. Anytime the individual subjective standard is preferred above God's objective standard, there will be a price to pay. Individualism is the worldview that causes people to think they are a law to themselves. Somewhere down the road, individualism will lead to either tyranny or anarchy. When people are committed to "doing what is right in their own eyes", they will find a gloomy ending. "There is a way that seems right to a man, but its end is the way of death" (Proverbs 14:12). Individualism is self-destructive. If anyone tries to convince you that individualism is the way to go, resist it for it is a deadly poison.

The philosophy of individualism flourishes in a political democracy. However, the aggregate of the individual voices is mass confusion and cultural chaos. Sometimes the concept of "an individual among the masses" is referred to in terms of a democracy. Isolated individuals, yes, but in mass they speak with an egalitarian voice. Egalitarianism allows the individual ethic to fit within the framework of the larger mass of society. Whoever has the loudest voice wins. The church that flirts with an ungodly culture will find itself being informed more by individualism than by the Word of God. If egalitarian tyranny prevails, the result will be cultural anarchy. It is true because the mass of individuals want to be equal in their wickedness. That was the problem with the

Benjaminites. Although only a few were guilty of the sin at Gibeah, they all participated in it by fighting for evil behavior.

The way to correct individualism, and every other "ism", is for everyone to do what is right in the eyes of God. Individualism will become dim if Christians find the framework of faith and practice in a covenant relationship with God. God's covenant people will repent of their individualism, if they come to understand that the work of Christ places them under His authority. Instead of promoting individualism, the covenant relationship with God through Jesus Christ should be the basis of community in the church and denial of individualism in the culture.

God's people must wake up and face the individualism and egalitarianism that is about to destroy the Western culture. Various societies are about to crumble as people clamor for their individual rights. When individual rights rise above the rights of family, church, and community, then lawlessness, corruption, and fighting will be the result. If individual rights rule over the biblical family, then the family will be destroyed. Many families in this country have long abandoned male headship and continuity in covenantal thinking. If individual rights rule over the rights of the church, then the church will soon be desolate of the truth. Many churches in this country are struggling just to maintain the fundamental truths of the Christian religion. If individual tyrannical rights rule over the God-given rights of the culture, then anarchy must follow. As for the state of this nation, it may be on the eve of collapse. Some churches in some European cultures are already plunged headlong into a neo-dark age.

The United States may collapse, but the church will not collapse. Christ is the King of the church. He will be victorious. The church is secure because the gates of Hell cannot prevail against it. Jesus Christ is the true King of

Israel; the Messiah, the Anointed One of God who lives and reigns forever. He is the only eternal all-powerful monarch that is able to confederate His people for community life in His kingdom.

During the time of the Judges, there was no king. Maybe they thought to themselves, "If we just had a king to stabilize our church and state? If we just had a king, he might bring order to our culture?" Then when God gave kings for His people, there was no stability and no order after the reigns of David and Solomon. Then the nation of Israel was cast into exile. Now what did those people think except, "we need a new king." We have a new king. Jesus Christ is our King. "For the kingdom is the LORD's, and He rules over the nations" (Psalm 22:28). It is time for the church to be re-formed by the Word of God. Then, and only then, the church will become the instrument of cultural reformation.

16. Cultural Reformation

Now the word of the LORD came to Jonah the second time, saying, "Arise, go to Nineveh, that great city, and preach to it the message that I tell you." So Jonah arose and went to Nineveh, according to the word of the LORD. Now Nineveh was an exceedingly great city, a three-day journey in extent. And Jonah began to enter the city on the first day's walk. Then he cried out and said, "Yet forty days, and Nineveh shall be overthrown!" So the people of Nineveh believed God, proclaimed a fast, and put on sackcloth, from the greatest to the least of them. Then word came to the king of Nineveh; and he arose from his throne and laid aside his robe, covered himself with sackcloth and sat in ashes. And he caused it to be proclaimed and published throughout Nineveh by the decree of the king and his nobles, saying, Let neither man nor beast, herd nor flock, taste anything; do not let them eat, or drink water. But let man and beast be covered with sackcloth, and cry mightily to God; yes, let every one turn from his evil way and from the violence that is in his hands. Who can tell if God will turn and relent, and turn away from His fierce anger, so that we may not perish? Then God saw their works, that they turned from their evil way; and God relented from the disaster that He had said He would bring upon them, and He did not do it.

Jonah 3:1-10

Cultural from the word culture refers to a particular way of life for a designated group of people. For instance, there was a time when the southern culture as a way of life was distinct from the northern culture. Modern technology and a passion for cultural unity have syncretized, to a certain degree, the two cultures.

In a culture with a majority of Christians, there will be a Christian culture to a greater or lesser degree. Therefore, the dynamics of Christian principles ought to be instrumental for the reformation of the culture.

The word reformation denotes a change from one way of thinking or acting to another way of thinking or acting. Biblical reformation is more specific. Biblical reformation refers to the church of every generation being reformed by the Word of God. Biblical reformation is not a *kairotic* event. A *kairotic* event refers to a specific event in time or a particular point in time that has great significance for the rest of time. Biblical reformation is a chronological engagement. Biblical reformation is not just about changes. Biblical reformation is a process that leads Christians to understand the nature and character of God in contrast to sinful man. It is a process that directs Christians to love the nature and character of God, so that their passion is to worship Him. For clarification, the term "biblical reformation" does not refer to any aspect of the order of salvation. Reformation is for believers who have been called regenerated, justified by faith and adopted into the family of God. Unbelievers cannot be reformed by the Word of God until God calls them and gives them new life in Jesus Christ.

One of the primary reasons for the absence of reformation in the church is from ignorance. The seed of reformation must be planted by preaching and teaching the full counsel of God. Reformation will grow when the believer discovers the truth and integrates it into his or her world and life view. However, there are many who have discovered the truth, but they refuse to embrace the truth. If a man has no concern or interest in truth, then the Spirit of God may not reside in the soul of that man. Obviously, reformation cannot take place if people are unconcerned about truth.

A disinterest in truth, reformation, and revival should be a concern to every Christian. The church that is not reforming will devolve its corruption to the next generation. Eventually the church will become so corrupt it will be called *Ichabod*, that is, the glory of God has departed. Unbelievers are not able to be reformed by the Word of God unless God the Holy Spirit changes the soul so they are able to believe. Wicked men will not seek reformation on their own. Believers are able and ought to express the willingness to be reformed by the Word of God.

The 16th century reformation was preceded by a corrupt, but powerful and influential church. It was through serious and agonizing inquiry into the Word of God that provoked Dr. Martin Luther to stand against the most powerful church in the world. The Roman Catholic Church had replaced the central teachings of Scripture with church tradition and the imaginations of men. The modern evangelical church falls prey to the same error by replacing the central teachings of Scripture with man-made doctrine and the imaginations of men.

At the beginning of the 16th century Reformation, Martin of Basle came to the knowledge of the truth of the gospel of God's saving grace. It was a personal reformation for Martin of Basle. Unfortunately, he was afraid to make a public confession. He wrote these words on a leaf of parchment: "O most merciful Christ, I know that I can be saved only by the merit of thy blood. Holy Jesus, I acknowledge thy suffering for me. I love thee! I love thee!" He removed a stone from the wall of his chamber and hid it there. It was not discovered until one hundred years later. At about the same time Martin Luther discovered the truth of God's saving grace from the Word of God. He openly confessed, "My Lord has confessed me before men; I will not shrink from confessing Him before kings." Martin Luther and Martin of Basle were both reformed by the Word of God and the power of the Holy Spirit. However, one invaded the church and eventually the culture with reformation, but the other buried reformation. An insincere reformation is no reformation at all.

The individual reformed Christian and the collective reformed church will take their reformation into the culture.

Jonah chapter three describes a cultural reformation. The book of Jonah depicts the true nature of reformation in the most universal sense. There may be a few preachers who actually talk about reformation, but they do not appear to take reformation very seriously. When they do talk about reformation, they are more often concerned with constraint and restrictions that limit reformation.

Since reformation is the recovery of biblical truth, Christians should hasten to bring it about. Recovering the truth of the law and gospel is ultimately important for the survival of any culture, because such recovery integrates spiritual truth into societal dignity and moral standards.

The next time you assemble to worship God look around the congregation and you will see the older generation is preparing to die, and the younger generation is getting ready to live. What will the older generation devolve onto the shoulders of the younger generation if the church does not seriously and sincerely seek reformation in the church? Biblical reformation affects every area of life including religious, familial, social, economic, and political life.

The book of Jonah reflects the principles necessary for reformation in church and society. Christians must be reformed by the Word of God, because it is necessary to grasp the true essence and substance of life and eternity. To ignore reformation is dangerous indeed, because without reformation God's wrath will be provoked.

From 1450 B.C. to 586 B.C., the people of God provoked God to the point that His glory departed from the temple in Jerusalem. It was symbolic of God's favorable presence leaving the people that professed to believe Him. God's view of a nation, a culture, or a particular group of professing believers is collective. Hosea warned the Old Testament church to "Take words with you and return to the Lord" (Hosea 14:2). Repent, and let the Word of God reform your mind.

Unreformed men will have no concern for the nearness, the uncertainty, greatness and eternity of God's judgment. The unreformed man will hear about God's wrath but it will not seem terrible or real to him. The unreformed man thinks to himself, "It will not happen to me." The unreformed man has a simple choice. He may choose reformation or judgment.

Jonah was reformed by the mighty hand of God before he went to Nineveh. Jonah's personal reformation required a little encouragement, but he finally got the message and found that reformation was better than judgment. The Ninevites experienced reformation because Jonah preached the full counsel of God. Every Christian and every generation must discover or re-discover the truth from the Word of God, so the beauty, majesty, and dignity of God will be the basis for reforming the culture.

Jonah went through the streets of Nineveh preaching a very simple, but very persuasive sermon. Jonah's message was, "Yet forty days, and Nineveh shall be overthrown" (Jonah 3:4). John the Baptist preached much like Jonah. They both preached repentance. Apparently, Jonah's preaching was very powerful and very convincing, because the whole city repented in sackcloth and ashes. The unexpected, but sudden reformation at Nineveh began with the people and very quickly reached the heads of state. The undeniable truth from the book of Jonah is that the reformation at Nineveh saved that city from God's impending judgment. "Then God saw their works, that they turned from their evil way; and God relented from the disaster that He had said He would bring upon them and He did not do it" (Jonah 3:10).

The sinful people at Nineveh were about to have the wrath of God poured out upon them. But God showed mercy after the people of Nineveh were reformed. God warns people of His coming judgment by means of sending a natural catastrophe, sickness, or other providential intervention that should get their attention. For instance, before the final destruction of Jerusalem in 586 B. C., God's people had little regard for the numerous lesser warnings that they received for nearly 400 years before God's fury fell mightily on Mt. Zion.

Sometimes God warns His people by warning other people around them with more severe judgments. The captivity of the northern kingdom of Israel was sufficient to awake the sinning southern kingdom to repentance. But Judah would not reform and so God's judgment fell upon Judah. Another way God warns people of His impending judgment is to send a messenger.

God has sent many a messenger to warn his people. Just as God sent Noah, Moses, Samuel, Elijah, and whole host of other prophets, God called and sent his ministers to warn first the church and then the whole world.

Jonah and the Ninevites experienced reformation and the people turned from their evil ways to avert God's threatened judgment. Later in the history of Israel, God spoke through the prophet Jeremiah and said, "The instant I speak concerning a nation and concerning a kingdom, to pluck up, to pull down, and to destroy it, if that nation against whom I have spoken turns from its evil, I will relent of the disaster that I thought to bring upon it" (Jeremiah 18:7).

God not only calls the church to reformation, which should be natural for the church, but God calls nations to reform. Once the church has recovered the truth of God's grace, the church must then take that truth to the culture. The present national sins should be of great concern to the church. Today God's people should feel the threats of every international, national, and local crisis that erupts. They should realize there is a coming economic calamity. The moral catastrophe that accompanies a "form" of godliness but not "true" godliness is obvious.

The only remedy is reformation for the church and the culture. Although prayer is necessary, it will not bring reformation. Although fasting is important, it will not bring reformation. Prayer and fasting are scripturally good and necessary, but they are not the instruments of reformation. A revival service without reformation is useless. The people of Nineveh believed the Word of God. This is the central principle of reformation, "they believed the Word of God." Then they fasted.

Like Jonah, individual believing Christians have to experience personal reformation first. Rediscover God's truth. The light of God's truth will light up a passion for reformation. Christians should not be ashamed of the same kind of preaching that accompanied reformation at Nineveh. "Yet 40 days and Nineveh will be overthrown" is a warning of cultural collapse. To try to hide the threats of God is like trying to hide from reality. However, Christians must not play the part of the well-intentioned dragon. The well-intentioned dragon is a professing Christian who says, "We know of God's impending judgment, but preaching God's judgment will chase people away and we'll never get to save them." Christians are so busy trying to save people, they fail to follow the commandment of Christ. Jesus said, "Make disciples of all the nations" (Matthew 28:19).

The majority of the church and most of our nation has not given attention to the terrible threats of God. God is angry about the gross hypocrisy and the great heresies that plague the professing evangelical church. The church will do well to listen to God's threat of judgment. The church will do well to cut out all the "talk" about reformation, and stop amusing themselves with egocentric worship. Talk and self-worship will find its end in God's judgment. The present condition of Christianity is that it suffers from a lack of understanding God's nature and character. The result is that the doctrine of salvation tends toward a form of universalism. The present unreformed church simply refuses to preach the simplicity of God's grace, man's sinful condition and in particular the doctrine of God's salvation. The fundamental doctrines such as God's justice and God's love have been distorted.

Since reformation is the recovery of biblical truth, natural man cannot recover biblical truth. Pray for the Holy Spirit to change the will of the natural man, so he or she may believe the gospel. Wicked men will not recover biblical truth, so God's covenant people are the only instruments of reformation. The culture will not recognize or accept the Christian worldview, until the church is reformed by the Word of God.

The apostle Paul preached and taught publicly to various cultures during his lifetime. On one occasion, Paul defended his ministry before King Agrippa, a Jewish King. Although Agrippa was trained in Judaism, his worldview was ungodly. Paul skillfully introduced Agrippa to the gospel and challenged his worldview. King Agrippa's response to Paul was, "You almost persuade me to become a Christian" (Acts 26:28). To a large degree, the 21st century evangelical church is an "almost believing church." The following are examples of the almost believing churches. They, like King Agrippa almost believe that God is sovereign, but not completely. They almost believe that the great Shepherd, the Lord Jesus Christ died for His sheep, but not completely. They almost believe that the Holy Spirit applies the work of Christ to the heart, but not completely. They almost believe that man is naturally dead in sin, but not completely. They almost believe in the biblical doctrine of forgiveness, but not completely. They almost believe in the biblical doctrine of worship, but not completely.

Theological reformation is the first order of business for the church. Every generation needs to be reformed by the Word of God. James H. Thornwell wrote one his colleagues July 24, 1846 about the poor condition of the church. His words are as applicable today as they were 166 years ago.

I am seriously afraid that the foolish liberality of the age will speedily plunge us into the same disasters from which we have just escaped. Our whole system of operations gives an undue influence to money. Where money is the great want, numbers must be sought; and where an ambition for numbers prevails, doctrinal purity must be sacrificed. The root of the evil is in the secular spirit of all our ecclesiastical institutions. What we want is a spiritual body; a Church whose power lies in the truth, and the presence of the Holy Ghost. To unsecularize the Church should be the unceasing aim of all who are anxious that the ways of Zion should flourish. (*The Life and Letters of James Henley Thornwell*, By Dr. B. M. Palmer, p. 291).

The church will flourish when she is reformed by the Word of God. The truth of God's Word is the catalyst for cultural reformation.

17. A Word About Worldviews

Christians should have some knowledge of how the various worldviews affect them corporately as a church and individually as Christians. It is the duty of Christians to formulate a world and life view that places the God they worship in the centerpiece of their thinking. Dr. J. P. Moreland explains the nature of a worldview: "A person's worldview contains two important features. First, it includes the set of beliefs the person accepts, especially those about important matters such as reality, God, value, knowledge, and so on...[and] a worldview includes the rational structure that occurs among the set of beliefs that constitute it" (*Kingdom Triangle*, by J. P. Moreland, p. 33). Worldviews are formed and confirmed by the way a person interprets the world around him or her.

A Christian worldview is based on truth. A statement like that provokes the question: What is truth? Theologians and philosophers in all ages wrestle with this question. Truth is that which is in agreement to that which is represented. Truth corresponds to reality, so you might say that truth is that which conforms to fact or reality. However, the postmodern concept declares all objective real truth is dead. Dr. Os Guinness observes that "in a postmodern world, the question is not 'Is it true?' but rather 'Whose truth is it?' and 'Which power stands to gain?'"

Christians have the Bible and understand biblical truth. Jesus manifestly explained why unbelievers do not understand biblical truth (John 8:43-47). The testimony of Scripture is, "The sum of Thy word is truth" (Psalm 119:160). Therefore, Christians ought to be affected by that truth. "Thou are near, O Lord, and all Thy commandments are truth" (Psalm 119:151). Moral truth will affect every part of faith and life. Moral truth is rooted in the integrity of God;

therefore, truth is an attribute of God, which He has chosen to share with His creatures.

I have tried to keep this book on a practical level. It was written so that Christian lay persons will be able to identify principles from the Word of God that will help formulate a Christian worldview. This chapter was added to help define various worldviews such as, theism, naturalism, secularism, humanism, materialism, consumerism, pragmatism, individualism, narcissism, victimizationalism, statism, and utilitarianism. This is not an exhaustive list of worldviews, but it will suffice for this brief survey.

THEISM

Theism is the fundamental world and life view of the Christian religion. Theism is the worldview that acknowledges a relationship to God in a personal way and that God's nature and character is what is claimed in the Word of God. Theism recognizes God as personally involved in creation and providence. It defines God as the only source of being, creation, and salvation.

NATURALISM

Naturalism is the worldview that denies the existence of a theistic God. Naturalism believes the Universe is natural and energy and matter is the substance of existence. Naturalism denies the spiritual nature of man. Sometimes referred to as scientific naturalism, it is the equivalent of atheism. Therefore metaphysics is out of the realm for naturalism.

Charles Darwin's evolutionary theory opened Pandora's Box for unbelievers and thus the arguments against supernaturalism. When this worldview hit the public square it influenced unreformed men and women to reconsider the theistic worldview. It has significantly shaped other worldviews. Naturalism requires no supernatural cause. Therefore it is self-existent and replaces God.

SECULARISM

Secularism is a worldview that encompasses many worldviews and is rapidly ascending in popularity. The western world experienced a rise in secularism, as a worldview, during the 20th century. Secularism is the most influential philosophy in the western world today. This is important for Christians to understand, because secularism is in direct opposition to Christianity. The tragedy is that during the last decade of the 20th century, secularism was widely accepted by Christians, because the church lost its message and meaning.

The root of the word secularism is the word secular. The word secular describes the here and now. "Live for today, because there may not be a tomorrow," so says the secularist. The aesthetic world, the world of media (especially news media), and the literary artists of our age are overwhelmingly committed to secularism. There is nothing wrong with the secular; it simply defines the present time. The conflict with Christianity is when the secular claims to exclude the eternal. Christians are interested in the present world, but their primary concern ought to be the eternal. The Bible teaches that Christians must be involved in the secular, but Christians cannot deny the sacred. Secularism excludes the eternal. Secularism not only conflicts with Christianity, but by excluding the eternal, it rejects Christianity.

The secular is inseparably connected to the sacred or the eternal. The danger for Christians is to profess hope for the eternal, yet embrace secularism and; therefore, reject the hope of the eternal. "For man goes to his eternal home while mourners go about in the street" (Ecclesiastes 12:5).

HUMANISM

The Renaissance of the 14th through the 16th century brought about a revival of "human" learning and a return to the classics. The rebirth of interest in classical literature and language along with the desire to revitalize culture and intellectual pursuits is said to be the source of religious humanism. Religious humanism found its way in the church through such thinkers as Erasmus, Arminius, and Locke. They believed that man was basically good and had great confidence in the power of education. These thinkers saw human rights as the vehicle to make good men, better men.

Over the course of time, religious humanism has evolved and has now become known as secular humanism. The American Humanist Association "asserts that the nature of the universe depicted by modern science makes unacceptable any supernatural or cosmic guarantees of human values." Humanism is inseparably connected to Secularism. Humanism is an enemy of Christianity!

Francis Schaeffer, an evangelical theologian and philosopher, said, "Humanism intends to beat to death the [Christian] base which made our culture possible." Schaeffer is correct! The modern humanist has a goal to destroy Christian ethics, morals, and values. They embrace the doctrine of man and deny the doctrine of God. The modern humanist believes that the supreme dignity for man is found in man himself. An ancient Greek philosopher named Protagoras has given the modern humanist a motto: "Man, the measure." Protagoras believed that man was the measure of all things.

Humanism has had a tremendous influence on the church. The impact is so great that Christians often embrace tenets of humanism, even while they remain unaware of the danger of humanism. How should Christians respond to this powerful worldview? Christians are the salt of the earth [and] the light of the world. "Let your light shine before men in such a way that they may see your good works, and glorify your Father who is in heaven." (Matthew 5:16). Humanism glorifies man, but theism glorifies God. Humanism is an ungodly worldview, but theism is a godly worldview. Humanism depends on the authority of man, but theism depends on the authority of God.

CONSUMERISM

A friend was very excited to find out that I had become a Christian. I remember him saying "you're still a salesman, you've just switched products." He was aware that I was once in the sales field. Out of my ignorance, I agreed with him, but I now realize that God is not for sale at any price or under any conditions.

The fundamental goal for most Americans is to be "happy." All of life is shaped around the desire to be self-fulfilled and happy. The French Revolution certainly had a profound influence on the concept of "happiness." Liberty, equality, and fraternity became the watch words that would bring the desired happiness to every successive generation. Do you want to be happy? The world view known as consumerism suggests that happiness comes from instant gratification. "Things" will bring happiness.

This is not just a philosophical worldview. Selling Jesus Christ has become an art among the majority of evangelical Christians. Evangelism is no longer God-centered, but rather it is consumer-centered. Even more significant is the loss of God-centered worship and especially God-centered preaching. When you go to worship next Sunday pay particular attention to your worship service. You may find there is more of a focus on entertainment, than on an infinite, eternal, all powerful, all knowing and ever present God whose character is marked by wisdom, holiness, justice, goodness and truth. All of these significant characteristics of God take a causal part in most worship services, if they are mentioned at all. Singers try to dazzle the audience with their sensational music. Preachers preach to "felt needs" using popular aphorisms, rarely expounding from the inerrant Word of God or using sound exegetical and hermeneutical skills. In short, entertainment is creating havoc within evangelical Christianity. Erich Fromm once said, "Modern man, if he dared to be articulate about his concept of heaven, would describe a vision which would look like the biggest department store in the world."

Holy Scripture speaks to the modern church: "You say, 'I am rich; I have acquired wealth and do not need a thing.' But you do not realize that you are wretched, pitiful, poor, blind and naked." Christians must put there trust in the creative and providential hand of an all powerful God. They receive and rest upon Christ alone for salvation and gain assurance of the power of the Holy Spirit in their lives. Take a few minutes to meditate upon the words of the Psalmist: "I have been young, and now I am old; Yet I have not seen the righteous forsaken, Or his descendants begging bread" (Psalm 37:25).

PRAGMATISM

Many worldviews have survived western civilization for centuries. Pragmatism is particularly an American worldview. The authors of this worldview popularized its philosophical theory by dismissing metaphysical rationality. Dr. Gordon Clarke defines pragmatism as, "A theory is true in proportion to its success; but success in solving a problem is eminently a matter of approximation" (*Thales to Dewey*, by Gordon Clarke, p. 503-504). To put it another way, the theory is true if it produces successful results. It applies to every level and segment of society because it is the final source of meaning and truth.

Although, pragmatism started as a philosophical movement, through the efforts of William James and John Dewey, it has become a popular worldview. If it works it must be right. The church growth movement has used this unbiblical worldview to promote church growth.

INDIVIDUALISM

Although individualism has a rich history, there has been a tendency to subsume individualism as an integral part of various classical philosophies. Modern man has taken this worldview and exploited it, especially the left wing politically correct crowd, so that individualism stands at the forefront among the contemporary worldviews. It's all about me and how I see the world!

The Greek city/state (the *polis*), the Roman ideal, the Renaissance, the Reformation, Modernity and now Postmodernity have all faced a certain degree of individualism. My thesis is that although individualism is a moving force within Christianity, it is not a Christian worldview.

Individualism embraces other worldviews such as secularism, humanism, pragmatism, and consumerism. Christians are certainly secular, human, pragmatic, and consumers. However, a Christian worldview places the importance on the sacred rather than the secular, the divine rather than the human, the truth rather than expedience, and the good life rather than the happy life. The Christian worldview places the emphasis on the sovereignty of God rather than the power of the individual.

Why have Christians rejected the sovereignty of God and favored the power of individual preferences? There are a number of factors. First, Christians have rejected orthodox Christian doctrine and theology. Secondly and related to the first, Christians have lost their passion for investigating truth. Thirdly and significantly, 21st century Christians are interpreting the Bible without considering the contextual, cultural, and historical factors. For example, the average person would say, "I have my individual rights as a citizen of these United (really un-united) States." The idea is that in a democracy the people rule. Throughout most of the history of the Bible and the history of the church, many people have been under some form of monarchy. The individual had rights only if the sovereign monarch granted such rights.

The Christian worldview is the only worldview that grants individual rights (de facto). Christians are the only people who are really and eternally given individual rights and at the same time Christians are under the rule of a sovereign monarch, the Lord Jesus Christ. Jesus said, "You shall know the truth, and the truth shall make you free" (John 8:32). A Christian is one who is adopted into the family of God and is an individual sibling among many siblings. It is the duty of all Christians to reject the philosophy of individualism and accept the sovereignty of God as the ruling principle in life.

VICTIMIZATIONALISM

One of the more popular milieus is victimizationalism. This is a passive worldview that was popularized by the therapeutic generation accompanied by a litigious society. It is a world- view void of any biblical understanding. The basic assumption behind victimizationalism is the goodness and worth of self. It is built on the unbiblical notion that "I am and there is not one else besides me" (Isaiah 47:10). This unbiblical destructive worldview essentially says, "When something bad happens to me it is the fault of someone else. On a practical level the alleged victim says, "Since it is their fault, they must pay me some money."

Now Christians, let's hear the rest of the story. The Bible says, "Each one is tempted when he is drawn away by his own desires and enticed. Then, when desire has conceived, it gives birth to sin..." (James 1:14, 15). The sin nature always puts the blame on someone else just like Eve said, "the Devil made me do it" (Genesis 3:8-13). The unbiblical therapeutic enterprise attempts to avoid the sin problem and dwell on the goodness of man. They would do well to dwell on the goodness of God and the badness of man.

STATISM

The Puritan revolt in England during the 17th century significantly contributed to an increase in political thinking and theory. Political theory captured the attention of philosophers like Thomas Hobbes and John Locke. Hobbes was an advocate of a sovereign state. Locke argued for a limited government. Both of these political philosophers found common ground in our American style of democracy. Our form of democracy has enslaved us to public opinion as a measure of truth. Any such idea was foreign to the Puritan mind and an enemy to the Puritan republic.

Allan Bloom in his book, *The Closing of the American Mind*, reasons that, "Although every man in a democracy thinks himself individually the equal of every other man, this makes it difficult to resist the collectivity of equal men." This however, is another danger in our American democratic system. The result of two centuries of American democratic federalism has produced the statism of our present day. Statism is the world and life view that gives the state all sovereignty and authority over its "collective equals." Webster defines it as "the principle or policy of concentrating extensive economic, political, and related controls in the state at the cost of individual liberty." The state then becomes the savior of those collective equals. Statism recruits egalitarianism as an accompanying worldview.

I pray that the Christians in this country will take heed to the dangers we face in the political arena. It appears that the majority of the people in this country have dismissed Christian ethics as a thing of the past. Political passivity among Christians is not the answer. Our elected officials are lauded for their immoral behaviorism. We must not be silent.

Christians must do two things. First, they must acquaint themselves with the contemporary political ideas so they can make intelligent decisions. Secondly, they must vote for candidates who are professionally qualified and possess common sense and moral characteristics consistent with biblical ethics.

UTILATARIANISM

Webster defines utilitarianism as, "The ethical doctrine that virtue is based on utility and that conduct should be directed toward promoting the greatest happiness of the greatest number of persons" (Webster's Encyclopedia Unabridged Dictionary of the English Language). This worldview applied on a personal level refers to using people to get what one wants.

CONCLUSION

The way a person interprets life and the world he or she lives in will end in disaster if the worldview does not begin with theism and end with theism. Every ungodly worldview has been identified in the Word of God. The most obvious is, "I am and there is no one else besides me" (Isaiah 47:10). Self-worship is the root of ungodly worldviews. Another ungodly worldview is, "everyone did what was right in his own eyes" (Judges 21:25). Self-worship invades the church and the culture. Finally, "In those days there was no king in Israel" (Judges 21:25). God could not be found in the church or the culture.

Now that we have identified the dominant culture, return to the King of kings, do what is right in His eyes, and call on the One who is first and last, the Lord Jesus Christ to direct your steps.

About the Author

Martin Murphy has a B.A. in Bible from Columbia International University and Master of Divinity from Reformed Theological Seminary. Martin spent nearly thirty years in the class room, the pulpit, the lectern, the study, and the library. He now devotes most of his time consolidating academic and practical gains by writing Christian books. He is the author of nine Christian books.

Made in the USA
Charleston, SC
11 May 2014